There's yan or tweea awd-fashion'd things
        Yan ommaist owt ti nooat,
Afooar they all git oot o' ken
        Amang t' new-fangled sooart.

F. W. DOWSON

LIFE AND TRADITION IN THE MOORLANDS
OF NORTH-EAST YORKSHIRE

LIFE AND TRADITION IN THE MOORLANDS OF NORTH-EAST YORKSHIRE

Marie Hartley and Joan Ingilby

Smith Settle

First published in 1972 by
J. M. Dent & Sons Ltd

This new edition published in 1990 by
Smith Settle Ltd
Ilkley Road
Otley
West Yorkshire
LS21 3JP

ISBN Paper   1 870071 54 9
      Cloth   1 870071 55 7

British Library Cataloguing in Publication Data
Hartley, Marie
Life in the moorlands of North-East Yorkshire – New ed.
1. North Yorkshire. North York Moors. Social life, history
I. Title   II. Ingilby, Joan
942.84608
ISBN 1–870071–55–7
ISBN 1–870071–54–9 pbk

Printed and bound by
SMITH SETTLE
Ilkley Road, Otley, West Yorkshire LS21 3JP

CONTENTS

PHOTOGRAPHS

DRAWINGS

INTRODUCTION

IT is twenty years since we started to research for this book which was first published in 1972. The region of the north-east moorlands (roughly the area of the North York Moors National Park) was until fairly recently an isolated part of the country which therefore had to depend on its own resources of nature and man for the manifold wants of farming and domestic life. As a result it was rich in crafts, farming practices and local lore, all of which have changed or gone. By means of recollections, fieldwork and photographs the book puts on record the old way of life of the moorlands.

In 1970 a very few horses were still to be found on the farms, but oxen had long disappeared. They were however very occasionally remembered, and it was remarkable to be able to record some of their names. Here and there harvesting proceeded in the old way with sheaves tied by hand, put up in stooks, followed by the animated scene of threshing. *Plates* 134 to 136 show the latter compared with the present day combine harvester (*plate* 137). On the other hand threshing by horse wheel is the subject of a unique photograph taken by us by chance in the 1930s in Farndale.

Peat was being cut for fuel and still is at the head of Glaisdale. A new thatcher has followed on to replace or repair the roofs of the numerous thatched houses. One of these, Oak Crag in Farndale, since we took the photograph (*plate* 10) has been destroyed by fire. Oak Crag had a witch post, albeit a faintly defined one, which could ill be spared. The rich folklore of witches, wisemen, hobs and fairies had been recorded by Canon J. C. Atkinson long ago, but we were lent two manuscript books by Major J. Fairfax-Blakeborough which harked back to deeply superstitious times.

A number of elderly people have died who shared with us their bright memories of how their grandparents, parents and they themselves lived. We still pay an annual visit to friends at Hutton-le-Hole and Kirkbymoorside. But sadly the Fairfax-Blakeboroughs are no longer with us. We occasionally see friends in Glaisdale, Farndale and Eskdale, and in all these visits we re-live again one of the most enjoyable studies of a great region in our working lives.

M. H. and J. I. 1990

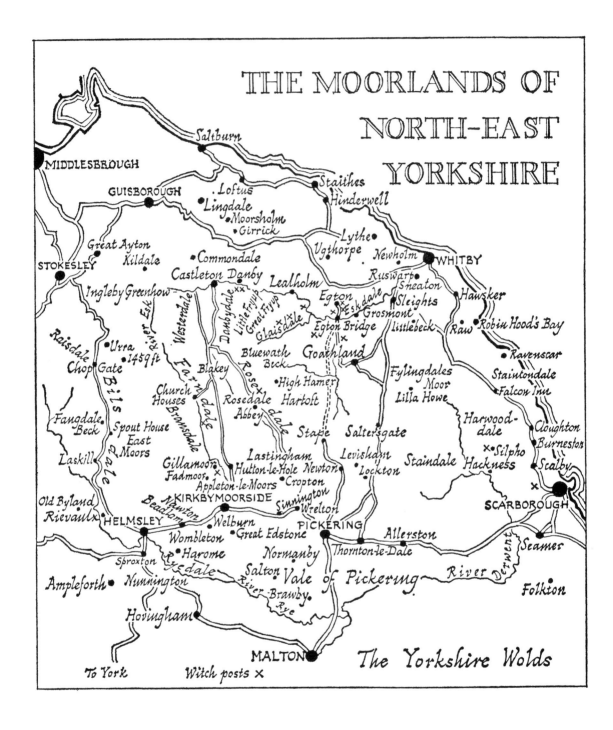

FOREWORD
& ACKNOWLEDGMENTS

WE have taken as the region for study the north-eastern dales and moorlands of Yorkshire, a compact area with a self-sufficient traditional life based on the natural resources of the country. The contrast between the region and that of the western dales of the Pennines, the subject of a companion book, *Life and Tradition in the Yorkshire Dales*, 1968, has been striking. Here, only separated from them by the Vale of York, are moorlands and valleys with a different geological structure, different resources, different farming methods, and a whole country of people with a different ancestry, different characteristics, and different local names.

Forming a background to the region are in the past the extensive natural woodlands, in particular the once great Forest of Pickering reaching northwards to Goathland, and at the present day the widespread tract of heather moor, stretching thirty miles from west to east. The moors, naturally divided across the centre by a ridge, and nowhere rising higher than 1,489 feet above sea level, diminish in height towards the coast. On the north side a series of small deeply indented dales run northwards into Eskdale, and on the south similar but larger dales wind southwards. Many ancient tracks, but few roads, join the two sides. Formerly the dales were far more isolated than they are now, and in all of them on farms spaced along the hillsides corn was and still is grown.

A saying runs, 'If a farmer comes down Saltersgate brow [that is, goes north] he's going the wrong way'. In other words better farming is to be had to the south, on the plateau between the dales and the Vale of Pickering, in the Vale itself, and on the Wolds beyond it. Outside the moorlands but inextricably linked, these three areas occasionally enter our narrative.

On the north side industrial Teesside lies only twenty or so miles from Eskdale, and in the past alum, jet, coal and ironstone mines were worked on the moors and the dales' sides. Centuries ago even pottery and glass were made on the moorlands. Industries are outside our brief. Nor does the coast, the eastern border of the area and a subject in itself, enter our story.

Although changes in ownership have occurred during and since the last war, this is a region of large estates. Three courts leet still function on the manors of

xiii

Spaunton, Danby and Fylingdales, two of which by courtesy of the respective lord of the manor and bailiff we have attended with interest.

As we shall show, within the lifetime of older men and women, not necessarily of great age, ancient farming practices have given way to those of the twentieth century. Versatility was the essence of the self-sufficiency of the moorland dales. 'If you want a thing, mak yan.' Similarly in the same short period the craftsmen of the villages and market towns have largely gone. 'They were all craftsmen in them days' and 'In the country you have to know a dozen trades' might well have been said of many.

One January day in 1969 we visited the Ryedale Folk Museum at Hutton-le-Hole to discuss our project with the curator, Mr B. Frank. From that day to the final stages of writing the book we have benefited from Mr Frank's advice and great store of practical knowledge given without stint. He also made available to us papers and letters on different subjects and the contents of this remarkable museum which we have used as a basis for the drawings. Later we were to meet Mr R. H. Hayes of the same village. He too with his wide knowledge of the district has given us generous support, suggested people to see, and provided us with an invaluable collection of his and his father's photographs. On the same January day we crossed the moors to Westerdale to visit Major J. Fairfax-Blakeborough. Again since then we have enjoyed a sincere friendship with him and his wife, and we have from time to time drawn on the major's lifetime's knowledge of rural matters and have been lent valuable manuscript books.

We should also like to thank those who are mentioned in the text and those who have posed for photographs. It would be repetitive here to list their names. We are also indebted to many to whom we have frequently turned: members of the Ainsley family, Mr Garbutt Agar, Mr E. Benson, Mr P. Burnett, Mr J. Davison, Mr C. R. Dykes, Mr W. W. Featherstone, Mr and Mrs A. Hart, Mr G. H. Leng, Mr and Mrs E. Mortimer, Mr and Mrs F. Raw, Mr and Mrs R. Smailes, Mr and Mrs H. Tindall, Mr I. Ventress and Messrs Frank, Bill and George Weatherill, of whom George lent us notes compiled by his father, Mr Jack Weatherill.

Others have given us information or introductions: Mr J. Agar, Miss I. Dunwell, Mr G. W. Goodall, Mrs C. T. Hyatt, Miss R. Kitching, Mr and Mrs A. P. Leadley, Mr and Mrs R. M. Pearson, Mr J. H. Rushton, Mr G. Russell, Mr E. Sonley and Mr R. Yates. Mr F. G. Payne of Llandrindod Wells has thrown light on the subject of the yoking of oxen, and Dr Anne Ross on the cross on witch posts.

We thank the curators of the Castle Museum at York and the Pitt-Rivers

Museum at Oxford for answering questions and allowing access to their exhibits, and also the archivists at the County Record Office, Northallerton, and the Borthwick Institute, York, the editor of the *Whitby Gazette*, the vicar of Kirkby-moorside, and the librarians at the County Library headquarters, Northallerton, the Central Library, York, and Malton for assistance. From time to time we have referred to a few books, foremost of which is Marshall's *Rural Economy of York-shire*, 1788. William Marshall, an outstanding figure in the history of agriculture, was born at Pickering.

We have stayed with Mr and Mrs B. Frank at Hutton-le-Hole, Mr and Mrs J. Sleightholm at Goathland, Mr and Mrs J. L. Thompson at Postgate Farm, Glaisdale, and for many weeks over the three years with Mr and Mrs J. W. Underwood at Kirkbymoorside, all of whom gave us an ideal background for work. When we started we little knew how many friends we should make in the valleys of the north-east moorlands, nor how much we should enjoy our sojourn, not least crossing the dark secret moors on homeward journeys to our rooms. As one of our friends said after a photographic session: 'It's all over like a wedding.'

M. H. and J. I.

January 1969 to December 1971.

PHOTOGRAPHIC ACKNOWLEDGMENTS

The authors have taken all the undated photographs from 1969 to 1971 and also those numbered 117, 194–7. Acknowledgments for the photographs with the numbers of the plates are as follows: Mr W. Hayes/Mr R. H. Hayes, 1, 11, 20, 37, 49, 50, 73, 75, 102, 109, 110, 131, 134, 136, 151, 154, 157, 163, 164, 233, 241, 245, 249, 250; Mr P. Burnett/Whitby Literary and Philosophical Society, 5, 6, 186, 192, 260; Rev. D. Adam, 7; Mr T. Watson, 12, 190; Mr F. M. Sutcliffe/Mr Eglon Shaw, 8, 51, 52, 53, 66, 74, 93, 99, 100, 104, 108, 184, 223, 238, 239, 251; Mr J. W. Collier, 38, 43, 76, 243; Mr J. Waind, 42; Mr J. W. Morley, 44; Mr H. Tindall, 45; Leadley family, 65; Mr A. W. Champion, 64; Mr S. Smith/Mrs S. Smith/Beck Isle Museum, Pickering, 63, 67, 72, 85, 132–3, 143, 202, 246; Mr Oxley Grabham/Mr A. Wilson/Yorkshire Philosophical Society, 69, 247, 248; Mrs J. Dobson, 71; Mr J. Tindale, 47, 54, 84, 129, 213, 219, 224, 257, 259; Mr C. R. Dykes, 87, 130; Mr W. L. Thompson, 88; Mrs W. D. Smith, 90; Mr H. Cook, 91,

203; Mr B. Frank, 92; Mr T. Page, 98, 262; Mr Oxley Grabham/Mr T. Lord, 112, 162, 179, 180, 181, 182; Mr I. H. Weighell, 122; Mr Eglon Shaw, 127; Mr A. Robinson, 144; Mr E. Benson, 145, 218; Mrs T. Cornforth, 152; Mr B. Unné, 169; Mr W. Holliday, 183; Miss L. Wilson, 185; Mr W. H. Swales, 193; Mr R. Smailes, 191, 204; Mrs A. W. Riddolls, 232; Mrs A. White, 240; Mr W. Tinsley, 242; Mr H. Dowson, 244; Scarborough and District Newspapers Ltd/Mr R. M. Pearson, 254; Mr N. Hutchinson for plan number one on page 3, and The Bilsdale Plough Company, Driffield, for the engravings reproduced on page 33.

ABBREVIATIONS

NRRS   North Riding Record Society
NRRO   North Riding Record Office
RFM   Ryedale Folk Museum
YAS   Yorkshire Archaeological Society

FARMHOUSES AND COTTAGES

SINGLE-STORIED, thatched and oak-beamed as they once all were, the old domestic buildings of the dales of the north-eastern moorlands, of which a number of examples remain, lack architectural style, but they exhibit instead antiquity of plan and construction of considerable interest. Although very many have been demolished leaving no trace, others rebuilt, and internal alterations have disguised almost all that are left, enough remain to show what they were once like.

These old houses form a definite group of vernacular architecture deriving in plan from the ancient long-house and in their cruck construction from the material at hand—the oaks of the forest where they were erected. Their sites, scattered in every valley, only clustered in villages on the outskirts, reveal their origin as *assarts* and settlements in the forest, and many of their names with only slight alterations have existed since time immemorial.

In late September 1860, when the men were working some distance away in the harvest field, the farmstead at Low Bottoms, Thornton Riseborough, west of Pickering, was destroyed by fire. The report in the *Malton Messenger* describes the dwelling house and outbuildings (stables, barns, cowhouses, piggeries, and a fixed threshing machine) as all connected together except for a small kitchen which was of later date at right angles at the back. This was roofed with tiles, whilst all the rest was 'very old and thatched'.

We have here a description of a long-house. Briefly, in a simple form, it was a single-storied building with the living part at one side and a byre at the other separated by a cross passage, which had front and back doors and entrances from it on one side leading into the dwelling and on the other into the byre. The cross passage formerly served as a feeding walk for cattle and as a threshing floor (hence threshold).[1] This disposition is the key to the basic plan of the old houses of the moorlands.

In *A Handbook for Ancient Whitby and its Abbey* Canon Atkinson (vicar of Danby from 1847 to 1900) describes primitive cottages seen at Egton. One had

---

[1] See Iorwerth Peate, *The Welsh House*, Liverpool, 1944; and 'Some Welsh Houses', *Antiquity*, vol. x, no. 40, 1936.

'one room with a clay floor, for the occupation of the family, separated from an enclosed place formed by boarded partitions which formed pig sty and calf pen under the same roof, by a narrow unlighted passage. . . . The family lived and slept in the same room, some sort of sleeping arrangements being contrived along the wall.'

These, the then disappearing old Cleveland 'cabins or cots', differed from the long-house/farmhouse only in that the latter was larger, of several bays, with storage space and eventually bedrooms under the rafters, and therefore more comfortable and hygienic.

Recollections of long-houses exist, such as Over Mortar Pits, built 1520, and Murk Side at or near Goathland, White House, Ugthorpe, Anthony House (now a barn), Westerdale, and others at Thorgill, Rosedale. The smell of cows and the rattle of their chains are remembered penetrating into the kitchens. Although much altered, examples of remaining old houses are: Oak Crag and Duck House, Farndale, Spout House, Broadway Foot, and Carr Cote, Bilsdale. Stang End, formerly at Danby, originally 74 feet long with five bays, has been re-erected at the Ryedale Folk Museum in its long-house form (*see pages 3 and 12 and plates 1, 2, 3, 6, 10*).

The canon continued his description of the 'cots' as having 'no sidewalls or at least low earthen banks as their substitute with the rafters forming the skeleton of the roof direct from the surface [of the ground] to the ridge-piece'. The roughly constructed *hemmell* with sod walls gives an idea of the ancient outside appearance (*see plate* 20).

The rafters described were crucks, a method of construction prevailing in the moorlands from early medieval times to the late seventeenth century. Formerly here called 'forks', they consisted of pairs of oak trees chosen to make an A-shaped framework curving upwards at first and then meeting usually to be joined together by a saddle supporting the ridge tree (*see drawings on page* 12). Each pair, placed about 16 feet apart, formed a bay.

References to pairs of forks occur frequently in the records of the Forest of Pickering.[1] Amongst other rights tenants had 'housebote'; and in 1336 for instance numbers of people were allowed 'payres of forkes', 'ribbes', 'bawkes' and 'creples' (possibly scaffolding). In 1518 the Abbot of Whitby took as many oaks

---

[1] *The Honor and Forest of Pickering*, vols I and II, 1894, 1895, ed. R. B. Turton, NRRS. For the distribution of cruck trusses and structure of cruck-built houses see: J. T. Smith, 'Cruck Construction: a survey of problems', *Medieval Archaeology*, vol. VIII, 1964, and J. T. Smith, 'The Evolution of the English Peasant House in the late seventeenth century', *Journal of the British Archaeological Association*, third series, vol. XXXIII, 1970.

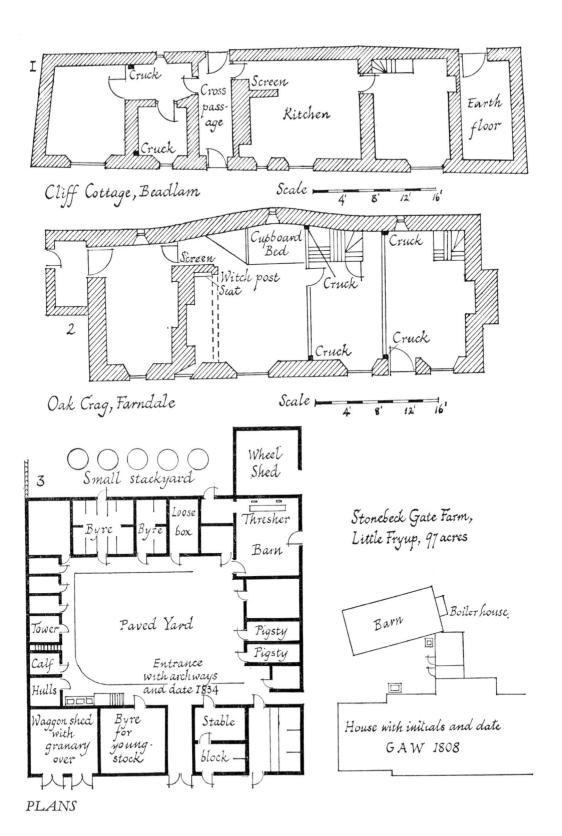

1

Cruck

Cruck

Cross passage

Screen

Kitchen

Earth floor

Cliff Cottage, Beadlam

Scale 4' 8' 12' 16'

Screen

Witch post Seat

Cupboard Bed

Cruck

Cruck

Cruck

Cruck

2

Oak Crag, Farndale

Scale 4' 8' 12' 16'

3

Small stackyard

Byre

Byre

Loose box

Wheel Shed

Thresher

Barn

Tower

Calf

Hulls

Paved Yard

Entrance with archways and date 1834

Pigsty

Pigsty

Waggon shed with granary over

Byre for young stock

Stable block

Stonebeck Gate Farm, Little Fryup, 97 acres

Barn

Boiler house

House with initials and date
G A W 1808

PLANS

in Goathland as made after 'the maner of the countrey iij pair of forkes'. In 1336 two houses, built in ancient times within, were carried without the forest—a demonstration of the ease with which a house might be moved; but no hint of the custom of a communal fork rearing has survived.

Some crucks of great age have been re-used either their full length or cut down to serve as upper crucks in upper stories, for, as described in Tuke's *General View of Agriculture of the North Riding*, 1794: 'The oak timber grown in great part of this Riding, though not large, is most excellent; produced as it chiefly is, upon sound and often rocky ground, its growth is very slow, which renders it extremely hard and durable.' But only a little earlier William Marshall had written[1] that 'oak is now almost wholly laid aside as a material for the house-carpenter except for door and window-lintels, wall-plates and some few other purposes'.

Cruck-built houses range from two-roomed cottages with one pair of crucks in the centre, for example Rigg House, Glaisdale (ruins), and the cottage at Egton (*see plate* 8), to single-storied dwellings with five pairs such as Stang End. There were also the rare two-storied cruck-built farmhouse at Wrelton which was pulled down in 1965 and the hall-plan Manor House from Harome with three pairs of massive crucks 25 feet tall, now re-erected at the Ryedale Folk Museum (*see plate* 22).

It does not necessarily follow that all cruck-built houses were long-houses; nor are thatched houses always cruck-built. Surveyed individually by Mr R. H. Hayes of Hutton-le-Hole, about eighty cruck-built houses, including those turned into barns and ones with upper crucks only, still remain in the dales, Eskdale and the villages bordering the Vale of Pickering.

In the second half of the seventeenth century many farmhouses were built with stone walls 6 to 7 feet high, still often cruck-built and thatched. Dated door-heads and mullioned windows, incorporated in later houses and barns in both Glaisdale and Danbydale for instance, point to considerable rebuilding. In that century a second house was sometimes erected close to one already there: there are two Spout Houses and two Laverock Halls in Bilsdale, and there were once two at Oak Crag, Farndale. Not many of these yeomen's houses have survived to the present day, and when a new house was erected later some were turned into barns as at Thorn Hill, Goathland, and York House, Glaisdale.

Built in 1606, Spout House, once the Sun Inn, Bilsdale, is an early and the outstanding example of the period (*see plate* 2), and is not a long-house but a dwelling of three bays with two pairs of crucks. When licensed in 1714 it took the

[1] *Rural Economy of Yorkshire*, 1788, vol. 1, p. 123.

place of an old inn formerly in Birch Wood not far away,[1] and in August 1914 when the new Sun Inn across the yard from it was completed, the old house was left unoccupied. It has a wide cross passage from which a ladder led to a bedroom, the kitchen/bar parlour with at the side of the fireplace a brick oven, and through the kitchen the low parlour, often used as a bedroom, out of which a stair curves up to two bedrooms each containing two box beds under the thatch—formerly the guests' quarters.

Besides Spout House there are twenty-five thatched houses still to be seen in the region.[2] Spars and lats of riven oak supported thatches of ling, *seaves* (rushes), sometimes bulrushes and bracken. But the thatching material recollected and used for houses is rye and wheat straw, of which a thatch of the former lasted twenty years and of the latter ten; and several thatchers, who often combined their work with running a smallholding, are remembered round Helmsley and Egton Bridge.

For thatching houses straw was first drawn by working all the short pieces out, laying it on two bands and tying it up in *loggins* (bundles), of which twelve made a threave. To count the threaves every twelfth loggin was thrown out, and another put in. A few days before use they were steeped in a pond or a stream. For a completely new thatch, the loggins were rammed hard between the spars and rafters and stitched down tightly, originally with straw bands. The thatch was shaved down, thumped with a *thack* batten and shaved again.

But usually the old thatch, scraped down and cleaned, was left on. In this case wisps of straw doubled over between the prongs of a swallow tail were stobbed in, about seven in a *breead* (a course) a foot wide, moving upwards (see *plates* 194 *to* 201 *and page* 6). After raking down from the top, the thatch was trimmed with a shaving knife, the straw being held down with a lat. If the site was a windy one, hazel rods, sewn down with band, were laid across and down the sides, and mortar, mixed with washing soda and chopped straw finished with a coat of melted tar, made the ridge. Mr Basil Ainsley, who together with Mr Isaac Ventress has described thatching for us, says that it takes 800 battens (loggins) to thatch Spout House.

From the middle of the eighteenth century onwards the old houses began to be replaced by two-storied, modest-sized, four-square, Georgian-style farmhouses,

[1] Information including date from Mr Jim Ainsley, whose family have lived for five generations at Spout House. He also states that there were once thirty-five cruck houses in Bilsdale, seventeen of them in lower Bilsdale.
[2] There are seven at Harome, six at Pockley, four in Farndale, two (including Spout House) in Bilsdale, three at Beadlam, one at Thornton-le-Dale, one at Sproxton and two at the Ryedale Folk Museum. Mr A. Agar remembers fourteen thatched houses at Egton in the early years of this century.

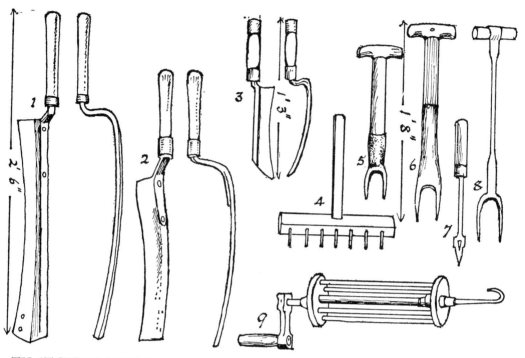

THATCHING TOOLS

1 and 2 Shavers. 3 Easing knife. 4 Rake. 5, 6 and 8 Swallow tails. 7 Thatching needle. 9 Straw rope twister.

mostly separate from the now more extensive buildings. The layout of the farmstead followed no uniform plan. Buildings were erected as convenience and the lie of the land dictated. According to Ord,[1] Francis Mewburn of the Howe, near Castleton, introduced the courtyard type towards the end of the eighteenth century. The outbuildings at the Howe remain and those of Stonebeck Gate, Little Fryup, are another good example of the plan (*see page* 3).

This era coincided with the introduction of a new roofing material—red pantiles, used for new and for re-roofing old houses. From about 1740 pantiles had been imported from northern ports to Whitby, where a tilery was eventually established,[2] and tiles were also made below Pickering. From a depot, the Tile Yard, at Cropton, four miles north-west of the town, they were carried into

[1] J. W. Ord, *History and Antiquities of Cleveland*, 1846.
[2] L. Charlton, *History of Whitby*, 1779.

Eskdale and its tributary dales.[1] Later tileries were started. In 1850 1,450 tiles from Loftus were supplied for £4 7s. for Lealholm Bridge Inn.[2]

Building continued into this century. Members of the Boanas family remember that whilst Plum Tree, Glaisdale, dated 1693, was being rebuilt, they lived in an outhouse, and masons recollect lodging in the old thatched dwellings whilst they were engaged on the new houses. Estate masons such as the Handleys of Farndale put up many in that dale at the turn of the century and the Weatherills built several in Raisdale and Bilsdale. The story goes that about 1860 a mason, Jack Wright, a very strong man, was offered by Lord Feversham a cow, or £11 and materials all found to build a house at Laskill, Bilsdale, of which it is said he chose the latter and put up the whole of the front in one day.

The names of the farmhouses reflect these changes. There are two Oak Houses in Bilsdale and one in Farndale, a Thatch House in Danbydale, and three Red House Farms in Rosedale, at Egton and north-west of Hackness.

[1] J. T. Sewell, *An Account of Some Medieval Roads*, 1923.
[2] NRRO, Vouchers, 1849–50, Viscount Downe.

EXTERIORS

1. *Duck House, Farndale, probably built by J. Duck, mason, about 1520. Renovated in 1957, it is no longer thatched. It has four pairs of crucks and box beds. The turf house on the left is a nineteenth-century addition, and a school used to be held in the other end (1908).*

2. *Spout House, Bilsdale, formerly the Sun Inn, has two pairs of crucks, cross passage, beehive oven and box beds.*

3. *Raw Farm, near Robin Hood's Bay, a long house with cross passage and blocked door in it leading to a barn. It is 107 feet long.*

4. *Beckhole, near Goathland, engraving by G. Nicholson (1821).*

5. *Poplar, Glaisdale, a seventeenth-century thatched house formerly on the east side of the valley. Pulled down prior to 1900.*

6. *Murk Side, near Beckhole, Goathland. A long-house showing the open doors of the cross passage which was here a public right of way. The house on the right had two rooms, the kitchen with a witch post and a flagged floor, and a parlour with an earth floor. The cow byre was entered from a door on the left at the far end of the passage. Pulled down in the early years of this century; the foundations of the house remain.*

7. *Lizzie Watson, known as Lizzie Haggaback, in the kitchen of the moorland smallholding of that name near Castleton. The turf fire burning at floor level was said not to have been out for nearly a hundred years* (c. *1910*).

COTTAGES

8. *Anne Heaton's cottage, Egton. Part is in ruin revealing a central pair of crucks (before 1900).*

9. *Moorland cottage kitchen range, Moorland Farm, near Sneaton. The two original downstairs rooms are partitioned by furniture.*

OAK CRAG

10. *Oak Crag, formerly called Great Oak, Farndale, a renovated and altered medieval long-house; 58 feet long by 23 feet wide. Three pairs of crucks. The 'dovecot' windows and the thatch are recent.*

11. *The parlour of Oak Crag, showing witch post with traces of carving and screen behind it with notch where seat formerly stood. The great beam on which are seen horse brasses formerly supported the smoke hood. On the right can be seen the panelling of a former box bed (1964).*

INTERIORS

AS in the western Yorkshire dales, 'firehouse' was one of the terms used for a dwelling house, referring to that part of the long-house with the fire, originally on a central hearth. When house walls were built in stone in the seventeenth century, the hearth was placed against the back of the wall of the cross passage and an interior plan with definite features evolved (*see plan* 1 *on page* 3).

The front door opens into the cross passage, and from it either on the left or on the right the kitchen is reached by a short passage formed by the outer wall and a screen or spear or *heck*, a partition of wood or stone, at the side of the hearth (*see plates* 11 *and* 13). This terminates in a post supporting a massive beam (at the other end let into the opposite outside wall) on which rests—or rested, for only one or two have survived—the smoke hood. Defined by the screen and the smoke-hood beam is a space by the hearth, 8 to 12 feet long by 3 to 4 feet wide, lighted by a small window. A narrow bench with an arm rest, sometimes stone (the *hecksteean*), is fixed to the screen in the *neukin* (the chimney corner), a position sometimes occupied by a *squab* (a cushioned sofa).

The smoke hood, tapering up to the chimney, was composed of wattle and daub (seen reconstructed at the Ryedale Folk Museum) or of stone, seen at Carr Cote, Bilsdale (*see page* 12). When there was no range and the hearth was on the floor, the chimney is remembered open to the sky and wide enough 'to hang a bullock up in it'. To avoid the ridge-tree, chimneys, supported on the cross-passage wall, had to be built a little lower down the roof (as at Houlsyke House and Hollins, Farndale). This feature as well as the small window near the fireplace are sure indications of the antiquity of a house.

In a few surviving cases the post supporting the smoke-hood beam is carved at the top, sometimes simply, sometimes elaborately with a cross (X) and usually with one or more rolls mostly below it (*see drawings on page* 9). In this century, not before, they have been called witch posts when so ornamented. Although no folk tradition exists, it has been surmised that the purpose of the cross was to afford protection against witches.

The known facts are that in the British Isles apart from one at Rawtenstall in

8

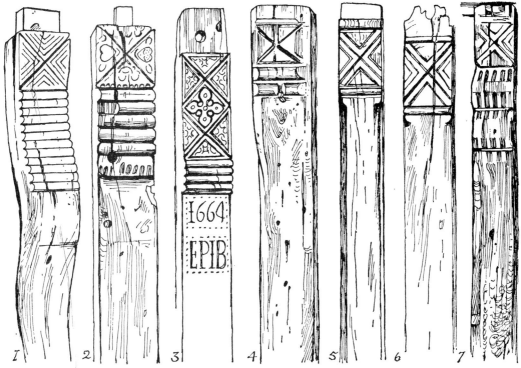

WITCH POSTS

1 From an old house in Danby (Pitt-Rivers Museum, Oxford). 2 From an old house near Scarborough (Pitt-Rivers Museum, Oxford). 3 From Postgate Farm, Glaisdale. 4 In situ in the house, Stang End, formerly at Danby, re-erected at the R.F.M. 5 From Low Bell End, Rosedale (R.F.M.). 6 From Gillamoor, near Kirkbymoorside. 7 In situ in Quarry Farm, Glaisdale.

Other witch posts are at Oak Crag, Farndale, Pond Cottage, Silpho (ill defined), one from East End Cottage, Egton (Whitby Museum), one with the top sawn off formerly in the old Murk Side, near Beckhole, now in the house near by, two replaced at Lanes Farm, Glaisdale and Bugle Cottage, Egton, three known to have existed at Danby, Egton and Wild Slack, Lealholm, and one covered up at Delves Cottage, Egton Bridge.

Lancashire[1] witch posts are to be found only in this area of north-east Yorkshire (*see map on page* xii), that they are a part of the structure of the house, that the wood is oak, and the carving is in seventeenth-century style. The one from Postgate Farm, Glaisdale, is dated 1664. Supporting the theory of protection from witches, one of the very rare cases in the church courts occurred in 1678 when Dorothy Cooke of Whitby was accused of bewitching a child to death.[2]

[1] Mary Nattrass, 'Witch Posts', *Gwerin*, vol. III, 1962.
[2] Borthwick Institute, York, R VII H 335. See also pages 122–4.

It would seem that the carved posts continue an ancient tradition carried on from medieval times and medieval houses, which may have derived the symbol of the cross from even earlier dwellings. The type of cross was widely used in the Bronze and Iron Ages as a solar symbol, a variant of the triskele, swastika and so on, and the background of extensive settlement by early peoples on the moorlands is to be taken into account. The use here of this ancient cruciform symbol implies a belief in its magical powers to avert evil and to afford protection against witches or any other hostile powers. The carvings on the post from Scarborough incorporate signs from astrology, a science widely practised in the Middle Ages. What the rolls signify is not known. The persistence of tradition may be noted in the crossed twigs formerly put over doors, and in the last and this century in the lozenges cast on oven doors, both forming a cruciform shape (*see plates* 12 *and* 16).

Let into the thickness of the wall at the side of the hearth near the little window were a spice cupboard and below it a salt box, both with small, often carved, oak doors on dowel pin hinges. The spice cupboard is a well-known feature, but this kind of salt box, like the witch post, is specific only to the region. It is formed by two hollowed-out oblong sandstone boxes without tops, a shallow one inverted over a deep one, with a small opening large enough for the insertion of the hand cut out of the front. Salt boxes are about 30 inches wide by 22 inches high by 16 inches deep outside measurements and are built flush in the wall. Although there are more, we have seen about twenty, often located in remote houses.

Their use is not remembered, but their origin appears to stem from the proximity to the coast where in the Middle Ages salt pans were leased by local abbeys, and Saltersgate, the salt dealers' road, between Whitby and Pickering, was so called in the fourteenth century. In the seventeenth century there were salt pans at Whitby, to which port salt was also imported, and it was brought by river from Hull to Malton in the mid eighteenth century. Delivered it may be supposed by donkey or packhorse, salt was needed in quantity for salting down beef, mutton, pork, fish and butter. Farmers used to supply salt beef to the sailing ships leaving Whitby the first week in March, and 'hung beef' is still remembered being eaten all winter at the formerly remote farmhouses in Hartoft.[1]

The arrangements in old houses are shown in the inventory, taken in 1699, of William Stead, 'slaywright' (sledwright) of Farndale.[2] His house had three bays, the forehouse with a cupboard, a table and frame and a clock, a middle parlour with two bedsteads and chairs, and a high parlour with one bedstead, a chest and 'other things', and a chamber. Beds, usually partitioned off in cupboards, generally

[1] Mr Allison Hutton, Fylingthorpe, and Mr H. Peirson, Hartoft.
[2] Borthwick Institute, York; Original Wills, Ryedale Deanery.

occupied one side of the rooms (*see plate* 11). At Murk Side, near Goathland, it is remembered that a bedstead had sunk so low into the earth floor that there was scarcely any space between it and the ground.[1] Earth floors, beaten down hard, were gradually replaced by stone flags, but they are remembered as being sanded to combat their tendency to become muddy.

In chambers under the rafters lit by tiny windows at floor level were a late seventeenth-century innovation, box beds, which still remain, although disused, at Spout House, Duck House, Farndale, and elsewhere (*see page* 12). As sleeping quarters, however, they are well remembered. When the wind blew, bits of straw fell down on to the occupants and wasps sometimes crawled in from a nest in the thatch.

Every farmhouse had, as some still have, a long scrubbed kitchen table with forms at either side, a grandfather clock, an oak chest, and an oak dresser with a rack locally made. But gone is the court cupboard or 'bride wain' (*see plate* 35) as it was called because it held the linen belonging to the bride and was carried in a wain to her new home on her wedding day. Described by Marshall in 1788, but already an event of the past, the ceremony included the wain drawn by ten or twenty pairs of oxen whose horns and heads were ornamented with ribbons, and with the bride sitting at her spinning wheel at the centre of the load. What a remarkable sight has been lost to us!

Bride wains are described by Canon Atkinson as 'fine old black oak cabinets' which in his early days in Danbydale were to be seen in most farmhouses, sometimes in old cottages. Although the wedding occurred before his day, he records that a bride wain was taken from Danby Castle to the church and on to the home of the newly-married couple on a wain drawn by sixteen oxen; the bride wain itself, some of its contents and the oxen were often wedding presents.[2]

Again in *Tom Keld's Hole*, 1880, W. Stonehouse pictured Christmas Eve in the late eighteenth century at the 'thatched, low-browed, whitewashed' inn formerly near Abbot's House, Goathland, where 'the furniture, particularly a richly coloured oak bridewain, had been beeswaxed and rubbed to a high state of polish'. Lastly going out of fashion, they were cast aside until the antique dealer arrived to buy them up. Hardly any remain in the district today.

The turf fires were famous, and when well-made, with a wet turf pushed into the ashes and a scuttle of turf mould thrown on, they kept in overnight. Many people, especially the innkeepers of the moorland inns, claimed that their fires had not been out for a hundred years. It was also customary to burn a 'clog' or

[1] Mrs A. Hollings, Goathland.
[2] Rev. J. C. Atkinson, *Forty Years in a Moorland Parish* (1891), 1923 edition, pp. 210–11.

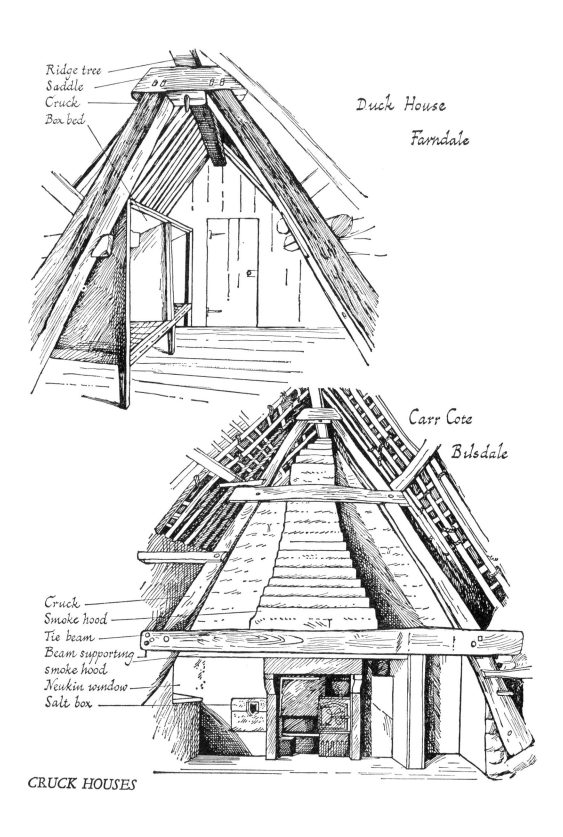

Ridge tree
Saddle
Cruck
Box bed

Duck House

Farndale

Carr Cote

Bilsdale

Cruck
Smoke hood
Tie beam
Beam supporting
smoke hood
Neukin window
Salt box

CRUCK HOUSES

'stick', a euphemism for part of a tree, sometimes pulled by a horse to the outer door. A 'stick' at Carr Cote is remembered reaching from the fireplace to the door. Hens perched on others. Propped on a stool or log or upturned pail at one end, the 'stick' burnt away with a scuttle of turf around it and was pushed up as required.

Although some houses had brick ovens, and bread was also baked by placing dough in the hot turf ashes, the characteristic cooking in the moorland houses and cottages was by means of a variety of pans over a turf or peat fire; this continued long after ranges were installed, well into the 1930s, until this type of fuel ceased to be harvested. Remembered as 'pan-and-lid' cooking, people speak of 'slinging the pan' and of the 'hang-oven' (*see drawings on page* 14).

There were the *yetling*, a round pan with a *bow* (handle), three small feet, and a fluted lid on which embers were heaped, used for baking bread and pies or for roasting meat along with potatoes and Yorkshire pudding, and cauldrons cast by the Carron and Camelon foundries in Scotland, in which broth, half a ham or a stone of beef might be boiled, or fat rendered down after a pig killing. Frying pans of various sizes for baking and frying were common, and because the implements for baking oatcake—bakstones and riddleboards—have survived, we know that oatcake was baked, but is long ago forgotten. Over the open hearths these utensils hung on a chain suspended from the *rannel-bauk* (the bar in the chimney), but when ranges were fixed, cranes and *reckons* (pot-hooks) were added from which to hang them.

In an entry in his diary F. C. Dawson, schoolmaster at Appleton-le-Moors, described a visit in 1842 to a house in Rosedale where

> 'a jolly turf fire presented itself on the hearth, with a large iron pot suspended above, containing, as we soon found, a portion of our coming dinner. We had not been long seated before a *few* broth was served out to us after the despatch of which we were introduced into the adjoining parlour and sat down to dinner. The first course consisted of plum pudding with brandy sauce and the second of hot boiled beef and ham with pease pudding after which a few bilberry and apple tarts presented themselves.'[1]

During the last century ranges gradually replaced the open hearth, the smoke hood and the brick oven. The Wrelton Works, a foundry in that village, run by Isaac Hartas from the 1840s and the Rickabys in the 1870s, supplied castings for the Rosedale mines and ranges for farmhouses and cottages of the miners. Joseph

[1] MS. diary lent by Mr C. C. Russell of Appleton-le-Moors. Note that although plum pudding was a party dish, it was a much plainer form of the present-day Christmas pudding.

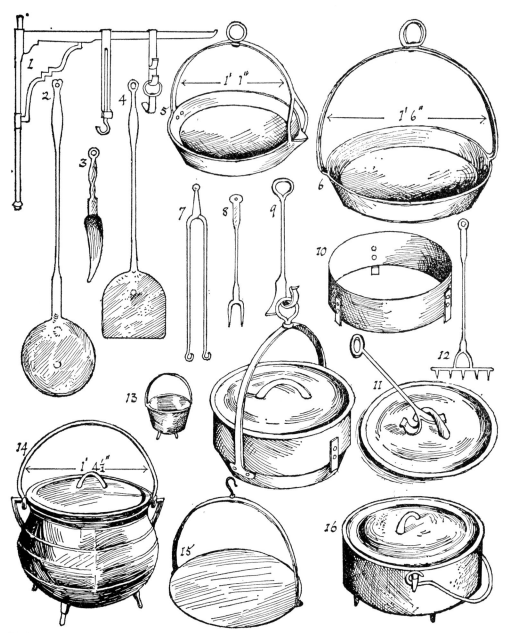

COOKING UTENSILS

1 Crane and reckons. 2 Oven peel (Danby). 3 Steel hearth tidier in the shape of the traditional sweeping tool—a goose's wing. 4 Oven peel (Plumtree Farm, Danby). 5 and 6 Frying pans to hang on reckon crooks. 7 Tongs. 8 Toasting fork. 9, 10 and 11 Frying pan used with sheet iron ring and lid. Reckon designed for lifting the lid. 12 Toasting fork. 13 Small iron pan. 14 Cast iron cauldron. 15 Bakstone. 16 Yetling (oven) either stood on the fire or hung over it on a reckon. (1, 3, 5, 6, 7, 8, 12, 13, 14, 15, all from R.F.M.)

Carter of Kirkbymoorside, iron- and brass-founder, made 'ovens, ranges, stoves, boilers cast to any pattern',[1] and Henry, his brother, attended the sale of the Wrelton Works about 1880 and bought the patterns of every size of oven door. As the other founders, Dobson and Fletcher both of Pickering and Robinson of Loftus, cast the same design of four lozenges on oven doors, it was common from Old Byland to north of Whitby.

Mr J. W. Carter (1888–1970), grandson of Henry, told us that he had made hundreds of ovens of both cast and sheet iron at the Cyclops Foundry in Tinley Garth, Kirkbymoorside. The cast-iron ones had fancy doors and the sheet the lozenge pattern. In 1920–5 they made a full fireside with a sheet-iron oven for £10 plus £2 10s. for fixing. Quite often ovens, replacing brick ones, were a separate unit in the wall a foot or even a yard away from the fireplace. Boilers were L-shaped or occasionally T-shaped (*see plates* 12 *and* 18).

A special feature added to the kitchen range was the hearth plate, a flat iron plate on feet which raised the fire about 5 inches from the ground. This had to fit each range and measured from 1 foot to 1 foot 6 inches in width and up to 6 feet 6 inches in length. It weighed up to 3 cwt. The grate, part of the casting that fitted into the recess between oven and boiler, had bars $\frac{1}{2}$-inch apart for a coal and $\frac{1}{4}$-inch apart for peat or turf. Sometimes the ash fell into a cellar, whence it was collected for spreading on the land. Very many have 'H. Carter' in raised letters on them, and they were still being fitted in the 1930s. Families enjoyed sitting with their feet on them.

The speciality of the houses of the moorland valleys was turf cakes made from 1 lb. flour, 3 to 4 oz. lard, salt, a teaspoonful of baking powder and half a cup of cream or milk. For pig-killing cakes currants and sugar were added. Baked as one cake in a large frying pan with a lid on, they were about $\frac{1}{2}$-inch thick and were turned with a knife and cloth after five minutes. Made for teas for visitors to the inns into the 1930s, they were then usually like scones, but either large or small, flavoured with smoke from the turf fire, split hot and buttered, they were delicious. One family we know still keeps up the old custom for Sunday breakfast of making a mixture the night before, and in the morning cooking warm cakes— eaten with treacle.

Whether called warm cakes, turf cakes, turn cakes, sad cakes, mell cakes, bakstone cakes, or pig-killing cakes, they were all a similar confection which, made at a moment's notice, were a part of the heart-warming hospitality of the moorland folk.

[1] *Malton Messenger*, 25th July 1857.

INTERIORS

12. *The kitchen of Dale Head, Westerdale, with a fireplace by Robinson Bros., Loftus. The boiler is L-shaped and the turf fire on the ground, with a toaster in front. On the right is a squab (sofa) and on the mantelshelf spills, irons, tea caddy and owsin tin (lading can) used for ladling water from the boiler (c. 1911).*

13. *Mrs K. Barker in the kitchen at Quarry Farm, Glaisdale, showing the witch post in position, the screen behind it and the door on the extreme right leading into the cross passage. The fixed wooden seat or settle was typical. The fireplace is modern.*

14. *Mr and Mrs R. Fishpool, Woodend, Westerdale. The range is cast-iron with a separate fire underneath the oven.*

15. *Mrs F. W. Holliday, Grange Farm, Stape, north of Pickering.*

18. *Mrs E. J. E. Harper, Skiplam Grange, near Kirkbymoorside. The range is an H. Carter, Cyclops Foundry, Kirkbymoorside, masterpiece. The separate oven was a usual arrangement, and the boiler is T-shaped.*

19. *Mr Bert Harper, Skiplam Grange, looks at a kitchen wall hung with rosettes and prize cards won by stock on the farm in the show season of 1970.*

16. *Mr T. and Mr R. Wheldon, Esk House, Farndale. A Herbert Carter range.*

17. *Mrs H. Agar and Mr G. Agar attend to cooking in a yetling with turf embers on the lid at North Ghyll Farm, Farndale. The range is one of Joseph Carter's, put in about 1880.*

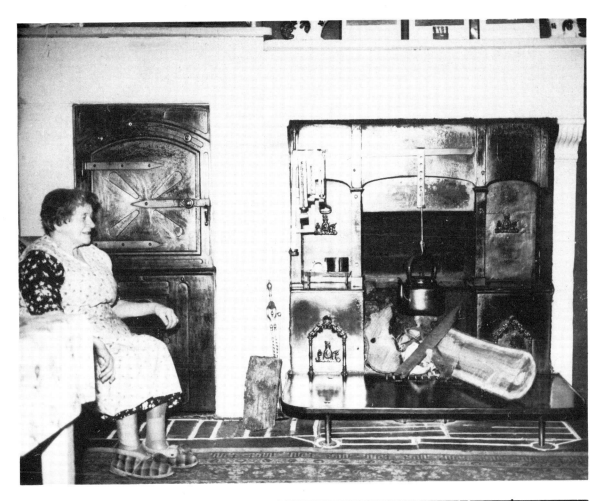

20. *Primitive shelter with sod walls. Ryedale* (c. *1900*).

HEMMELLS AND CRUCKS

21. *Hemmells (stone bases for supporting stacks) at the back of Old Kiln, East Moors, near Helmsley.*

22. *The Manor House from Harome in process of re-erection at the Ryedale Folk Museum, showing the three pairs of crucks.*

FARM SERVANTS

THE annual statute hirings, attended by labourers for centuries, ceased alto-gether after the passing of the Agricultural Wages Act in 1924. In the north-east moorlands and adjacent parts thousands of men and women had habitually changed their places of work where they had lived each year. Hirings were held at Martinmas in November at Egton, Guisborough, Whitby and Castleton, and on the south side of the moorlands at Malton, Pickering, Helmsley and Kirkby-moorside. If not engaged at one hiring the workers went on to the next, until having found a place and agreed on a wage for the year they were given their *arles*, a 'Godspenny', formerly 1*s.*, the 'fest' or fastening penny that sealed the bargain. Within recollection this was 2*s. 6d.*, and towards the end 5*s.* or 10*s.* They were then free to enjoy the fair, the usual accompaniment of hirings, and a holiday during Martinmas week before going to their new situations.

By the mid nineteenth century the system was under stress. The spirit of im-provement abroad in agriculture resulted in a stirring of social conscience, ex-pressed in *The Agricultural Labourer as he really is; or Village Morals in 1854* by the Rev. J. Eddowes, vicar of Garton-on-the-Wolds, who likened hiring day to a slave market.[1] It was taken up by enlightened farmers, in editorials in the *Malton Messenger*, and in reports in that paper of meetings of the newly formed local agricultural societies, all pressing for change.

The custom of hiring for fifty-one weeks it was said engendered 'a natural wish to change', and the practice of servants going from fair to fair trying to obtain the best wages and giving back their original hiring pennies was deplored. A concourse of people took their stations whatever the weather in a portion of ground seemingly allotted for 'the statty' like so many cattle open for inspection. Here came the farmer's wife with an appraising eye and the farmer who, actually handling a candidate, felt his muscles, spanned his wrists and surveyed him from top to toe 'doubtless reckoning how much work can be got out of him and how much he will eat'.[2]

[1] *Malton Messenger*, 1st April 1854.
[2] *Malton Messenger*, 29th November 1856.

16

Attacks were levelled at the attendant evils: the prevalence of pickpockets, the bad language, 'the miserable enticements of the Penny Theatres with objectionable scenes'. Besides these the labourers spent their Godspennies and more on wild beast shows, conjurors' booths, and at the public houses which they frequented for want of anywhere else to go. Drunken orgies had 'consequences which may be guessed'.

The farmers were the capitalists of the system with their own economic problems. It was said that a few literally worked their servants to death by sending boys into the fields in rain and snow.[1] Owing to outdoor work in bad weather in winter, it was not uncommon even until comparatively recently to see men and women, including the farmers themselves, bent double with rheumatism in old age. As for female servants, they were up earliest and on foot all day. None the less, ample food is mostly remembered. At Skiplam Grange the butcher called every day,[2] and rhubarb, gooseberry and apple pies followed in season.

In 1855 the opening of a registry office for women in Driffield reduced the number of women attending the Malton Hirings,[3] where 5,000 women and 10,000 men had usually assembled. Two years later another step forward was the provision of 'parchment characters' enclosed in a tin case, at the price of 6d., in which the farmer described his servants' conduct and sphere of work. It was suggested that farmers should have characters themselves.

In the late eighteenth century Marshall had noted that wages, £12 to £15 a year for an able manservant, were high, living was low, and working hours were long. By the mid nineteenth century at Malton Hirings a foreman's yearly wage was £25, a waggoner's £18, plough lads' £14, women's £15, those of secondary abilities £11 and young lasses' £1. In 1857 the attendance at Whitby Hirings was large but high wages left many without engagement. The figures quoted above continued without much change in the moorland valleys up to the First World War. After that they increased rapidly—£35 for a good man.

In the same period the servants themselves, especially young men and young couples with neither money nor prospects, dissatisfied with wages and housing conditions and finding the demand for labour threatened by the new implements, were making their own decisions. From the 1830s up to the 1890s thousands of them emigrated.

Week by week advertisements appearing in the local newspapers gave the names of ships sailing from Whitby to Quebec and from Liverpool to Australia,

[1] *ibid.*
[2] Mr I. Ventress.
[3] *Malton Messenger*, 8th December 1855.

America and 'the Canadas'. Details of rates of passage were available over the counters of grocers' shops at places such as Pickering, Thornton-le-Dale, Helmsley and Grosmont. For as little as £6 6s., even £3 10s. for steerage in sailing ships, it was possible to emigrate to Canada.

Before the coming of the railway young people walked to Liverpool. Craftsmen sold up their stock and left. F. C. Dawson described an early morning scene at Appleton-le-Moors in July 1843 when the blacksmith, Robert Shepherd, and his family set out by waggon for Hull, whence they were going to London to sail for Australia.[1] 'After 7 we . . . at length saw the whole family—father, mother & 11 children—coming slowly along on the other side of the road with many of their most intimate friends and acquaintances in their rear. The sight was an affecting one, for they were nearly all weeping.' Thousands from Cleveland went to North America and named Cleveland, Ohio.[2] The flood of emigration continued spasmodically into the twentieth century, then gradually subsided.

In the moorland dales hired servants enjoyed more personal treatment than that on large farms. The staff was smaller, so that men and women lived with the family and shared the same food. A rhyme that circulated in the old days runs:

> *Tha call ma Johnny Clagclod,*
> *Ah cums fra Danby Deeal,*
> *Ah's i' pleeace wiv a farmer,*
> *Ti plew an' swing a fleeal,*
> *Ti tent his flocks, and leeak ti t'kie,*
> *Ti hedge, an' theeack, an' stack,*
> *Ti be a handy farmer's lad*
> *At any kin' o' mak.*[3]

Hirings are remembered but not with the shepherd displaying a tuft of wool in his hat, or horsemen, waggoners and thoddies (third men) with a piece of whipcord round their billycock hats or a whip round their necks looped under their left arms.[4] Farm lads used to make lovers' knots, made of two plaits of straw twisted over, for buttonholes.[5]

Mr F. Raw has described to us the procedure in Fryup and at the hirings at Egton held on 5th November sixty or seventy years ago. Here men usually stayed

---

[1] MS. diary of the then schoolmaster, lent by Mr C. C. Russell of Appleton-le-Moors.
[2] G. M. Tweddell, *People's History of Cleveland*, 1872–6.
[3] MS. notes of R. Fairfax-Blakeborough.
[4] K. McManners, *Sinnington Through the Ages*, 1954.
[5] Mr J. Welford, Newholm.

two years, but it was possible to lose foreman, horseman and lad at a clean sweep. As Martinmas approached the master asked a man, 'Is t'a stoppin' on?' If he was he still had a day off to go to the hirings.

On the previous Sunday the lads in Fryup went into the woods to cut themselves hazel sticks to walk with; then on the day perhaps fifteen of them met at the Raws at Ajalon Farm and walked together to Egton. Here they sauntered up and down on one side of the street whilst the farmers gathered together on the other. Seeing a boy he liked the look of a farmer went up to him and enquired, 'Now lad are ye wantin' hiring? Where do yer live?' The wage was discussed, and if agreement was reached the farmer gave the boy his hiring penny. He was then 'fested'.

Wages were not paid until the following Martinmas at the end of the year's work. But in between the hired man or woman could ask for a 'sub' or 'subs', small sums that were deducted at the end of the year. On Martinmas Day a man worked until dinner time, and was paid as he walked out.

At Egton there were stalls selling sweets and fruit, coconut shies, and shilling dinners of roast beef, Yorkshire pudding, apple pie, and a cup of tea, put on at the Fox and Hounds. At Kirkbymoorside the town was packed with people so that 'you could have walked on their heads', and also with Alf Payne's roundabouts and fair organs, hoop-la, and other stalls.

After he was hired for the first time a lad was taken by his mother to the tailor's, from whom she bought shirting and knitting wool. Mr A. Leadley, who followed his father and for many years had a tailoring business in Kirkbymoorside, remembers that they kept open house for their customers from 11 a.m. onwards, providing a dinner and later a tea. His father, putting a hand on a lad's shoulder, used to say, 'It's all reet mi lad; I know t'breed.' He meant that he understood that clothes ordered for the year, including the ever popular good blue serge suit, costing 50s., and probably a summer suit bought at Whitsuntide, would not be paid for until the following Martinmas Day. Similarly the cost of the boy's boots from the cobbler or his weekly washing amounting to £1 for the year were settled up at the end.

Mr C. R. Dykes says: 'Nobody had underclothes. You always slept in a shirt. You had an extra one in case one got wet, and of course a Sunday shirt.' No one either had a collar, but instead wore a neck tie, a white silk handkerchief tied in a sailor's knot. 'T' aud people', recalls Mr H. Peirson, Hartoft, 'fastened a band round their trousers below the knee; they called 'em yokes. They took the weight off the trousers.'

Mr J. W. Newton of Beckhole, Goathland, born at Levisham, was one of nine children who were sent out to work as soon as possible. Just before his twelfth birthday about 1900 he was hired to a relative for three months from 15th August until Martinmas and, paid 2*s*. a week, earned 30*s*. in all. 'Coming from home,' he said, 'the food seemed terrible.' For breakfast it was sometimes porridge, but usually fat bacon and lumps of cold beef, perhaps a hot rabbit pie for dinner, and about six at night a basinful of milk.

He was next hired by another relative at Hawsker where he earned £5 the first year, £6 the second and £7 the third. This was a milk farm with a round in Whitby. They were up at 5 a.m. in summer and 6 a.m. in winter. Milk was ¾*d.* a pint and 'many an old lady bought a happorth'. Morning and night they had to go even with snow 'heaven's high'. In haytime, called out at 3 a.m., he often fell asleep turning hay on a tedder. On Saturday nights he might walk into Whitby. 'It was hard on a lad.'

It was not easy either for young women. Many a time a young girl might walk to Whitby Hirings. If she was not engaged she had to walk home to an isolated village at night, and was scolded by her parents for not having found a job. Mr Isaac Ventress tells how his wife before she was married was hired on a farm about the turn of the century. Up each day at 6 a.m. she worked until 10 o'clock at night, and earning £5 for the year 'never drew a penny of it and sent it all to her mother'. 'Other girls', he said, 'worked in the big mansions night and day.'

When she was twelve in the 1890s Mrs J. W. Scales was hired on a farm at Littlebeck, and similarly worked a long day. She fed calves, pigs, hens, picked potatoes, and for nearly three months of the year was in the hay or harvest fields. Although Tuesday was broth day with the broth boiled in a cauldron and eaten from basins, they had plenty of meat and bacon. At 6 p.m. they had cold meat, cakes and pies. 'Meat was cheap then.' The first year she was paid £5, but by the time she left to be married she was earning £13 a year.

Women used yokes for everything—water, milk, potatoes—'I remember one', says Mr F. Dawson (b. 1889) of Newholm, 'carrying two tiny children in pails on a yoke. Women sweated in the fields, and the children had to follow them about like little animals.'

Mr A. Agar, Egton, recalls that the last time he was hired was during the First World War when he went to work for a widow 'who was a proper man-woman and could hold her own with anyone. She gave me a big wage—£2 a week'. Later when he worked for his father-in-law, if he wished to stay up late he was told, 'Merry nights, sorry mornings, and work still to do.'

'At first', says C. R. Dykes, who was one of a family of thirteen and who started work at thirteen on a big Wolds farm in 1908, 'it was hard, but after a couple of years and a bit o' strength you enjoyed it. The routine and discipline larnt us civility.' He himself progressed, as it was possible to do by careful saving and good luck, from hired man to *daytal* man to taking a farm, in his case in Bilsdale.

The hired man was unmarried and lived on the farm where he worked. When he married he had two choices. He might make an arrangement with the farmer and go into a tied cottage, pay no rent, receive milk, keep a pig and a few hens and remain a hired man; or he became a daytal man, originally a worker paid by the day, latterly by the week, and who although enjoying less security, earned more. Daytal men formed a group quite separate from the hiring system. They each had their own cottage, perhaps a cowkeeping place or even a smallholding with a few cows, pigs and hens and often a mole-, rat- or rabbit-catching business. Sometimes they worked for a neighbouring farmer who provided their food and lent a horse when required. But usually they did 'a lot o' tak' (piece work). Many daytal men travelled from farm to farm, and specialized in, say, sheep washing, walling, thatching or mowing.

The daytal men, craftsmen, smallholders and cowkeepers of the moorland dales had for centuries provided a pool of mobile labour at the periods of peak demand —haytime and harvest. For the harvest there were in fact special hirings. As Henry Best records from the Wolds in 1641: 'The usual custom is to send to Malton and there to hire Moore-folkes, the Satterday following after that we are beginne to sheare' (cut with a sickle). His mowers were fed and paid 2s. 6d. a week. In 1856 at the Pickering harvest hirings mowers were offered 18s. to 20s. a week, gatherers 14s. to 16s., binders 12s., band-makers 3s. to 4s. per week, with board and lodging.

Many followed on from haytime in the Vale of York to that in the Pennine dales, and from early harvest on the Wolds to their own later harvest in the eastern dales. 'You had to find your bread where you could.' Between 1880 and 1900 Mr Job Todd of Hutton-le-Hole used to walk over the Hambletons finding work 'in the bottoms' (in the Vale of York), then, lodging rough on the way, went up to Wensleydale. Eventually he landed at Chapel-le-Dale in July ready for haytime, and when that was over took the train back ready for work at harvest.

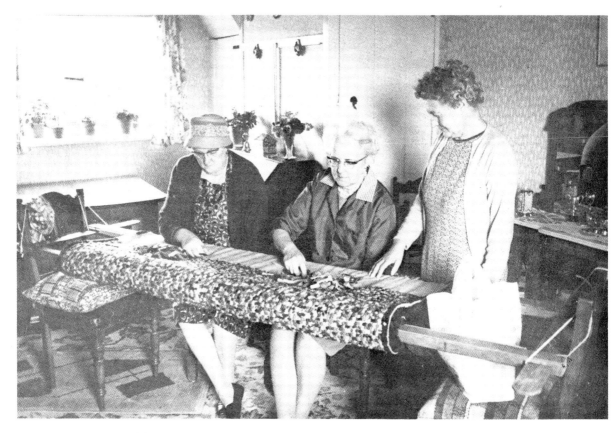

WORK IN THE HOME

23. *Mrs O. V. Medd, Mrs G. D. Medd and Mrs H. Williamson, Castleton, making a clip rug.*

24. *Mrs B. E. Knaggs, Westerdale, with quilting patterns.*

25. *Mrs B. E. Knaggs formerly made quilts but here quilts a cushion cover. Mrs S. Beeforth threads a needle.*

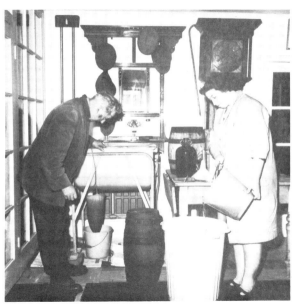

WORK IN THE HOME

26. *Mrs M. Graham, Hunt House, Goathland, pours boiling water on to a bunch of gale to make gale beer.*

27. *Mr and Mrs R. E. Garbutt, Low Mill, Bilsdale, making botchet (mead) with modern equipment.*

28. *Mrs T. S. Richardson, Helmsley, stitching together a quilt made of octagonal pieces of material.*

29. *Miss H. Adamson, Staithes, sews a Staithes bonnet, and Mrs F. Berrill looks at a pattern.*

BUTTER-MAKING

30. *Miss C. Atkinson, Raw Farm, near Robin Hood's Bay, churns cream for making butter in an end-over-end churn.*

31. *Miss Atkinson washes and weighs pounds of butter before making up.*

32. *Mrs D. Tyreman, Danby, making butter for Danby Show.*

33. *Miss M. Mortimer, Dale View, Westerdale, demonstrates using a barrel churn.*

34. *A typical dresser and rack, made by John Tomlinson (1841–1900) of Appleton-le-Moors.*

35. *Bride wain, dated 1678, probably belonging to the Danby district.*

36. *Eighteenth- and nineteenth-century Whitby gingerbread moulds. (Whitby Museum.)*

GROUPS

37. *Re-making Overscar Pond, Lockton,* c. *1910. Layers of lime, clay and straw are finished off with a layer of small broken stones as shown. Water with which to mix the material was brought from a quarter of a mile away in the water cart seen on the right. The pond dates back to the thirteenth century, and although overgrown may still be seen on the Whitby–Pickering road just north of the Fox and Rabbit.*

38. *The garden staff of Duncombe Park grouped on the East Temple steps. The hierarchy is obvious from the head gardener, Rochford, down to the women, the sweepers-up of leaves* (c. *1870*).

39. *A saw pit at Middle Head, Farndale. Mr J. W. Aconley, the top sawyer, using a whip saw, and Mr R. Frank, the bottom sawyer, demonstrate its use.*

40. *The base stone of a beam press under an oak tree near Mountain Ash Farm, Glaisdale.*

41. *Ox bow stone for making hazel bows for bullock collars, originally near Dale Head Farm (only foundations remain), Farndale Head. Three sizes could be made. Now at the R. F. M.*

STOCK ON THE FARM

DURING the latter part of the eighteenth century the changeover from oxen to horses for draught began, and arguments as to their respective merits ranged backwards and forwards for a century until the use of oxen as beasts of burden had ceased. Marshall puts the case better than anyone. 'Formerly four or five oxen in yokes led by two horses, also double, were the invariable "draught" or team of the country, not only upon the roads but in ploughing.'[1] He adds that when going uphill they were a sheet anchor and that they could be worked every day for longer hours than horses. Nevertheless the invention of lighter ploughs and the improvements to roads, making them stony and unkind to cloven hooves, spelled the decline in their use.

In the dales the use of oxen was common up to the 1860s, but thereafter they gradually ceased to be worked.[2] Especially in Eskdale they were used for drawing loads of stone—as witness the sight that greeted Canon Atkinson on his way to Danby in 1847 of a team of ten oxen and ten horses dragging a stone waggon up the steep bank at Stonegate near Lealholm.[3]

Rose and Ruler, two big Shorthorn-type animals, were employed by the Watsons of Longstone Farm, Sneatonthorpe, near Whitby, for leading turf from near Lilla Howe.[4] Rook and Bullet,[5] Jewel and Wanton[6] are other recorded names in the district. Tug, Lug, Hawl and Crawl were four famous oxen, which were not a success, employed in 1813 by the Reverend Sydney Smith, the wit, scholar and letter-writer, when building his parsonage house at Foston-le-Clay fourteen miles south of Kirkbymoorside.[7]

Besides several other similar recollections, a pair of oxen with a horse harnessed

---

[1] W. Marshall, *The Rural Economy of Yorkshire*, 1788, vol. I, pp. 260–7, vol. II, pp. 182–90.
[2] Recollections of Dr J. L. Kirk; and Isaac Cooper, *Helmsley or Reminiscences of 100 Years Ago*, 1887.
[3] Rev. J. C. Atkinson, *Forty Years in a Moorland Parish* (1891), 1923 edition, p. 39.
[4] Mrs E. Smith, daughter of Parker Watson who kept oxen.
[5] *Ralph Ward's Journal*, YAS Record Series, vol. CXVII, 1951.
[6] Alice Hollings, *Goathland*, 1971, p. 27.
[7] Lady S. Holland, *A Memoir of the Reverend Sydney Smith*, 1887.

22

ahead of them, a usual arrangement for they inclined to wander, is remembered at Abbot's House, Goathland, and oxen were used to plough almost to the top of Round Hill, Fryup. The *owse hoose* (ox house) was a feature of farm buildings as ox yokes and poles, always used because oxen liked to pull with a weight on their shoulders, were part of the equipment of a farm (*see page* 111). Towards the end 'ya beeast and a hoss' frequently made a draught for ploughing and other work.

The shoeing of oxen depended upon the individual farmer's finances, and if used only in fields they were not shod at all. Some farmers shod all four feet, others the forefeet and many only on the off side clove of the hoof, because oxen 'strike' on that side. For shoeing they had to be flung, that is laid on their sides in the smithy, and special stocks to hold them have only recently been destroyed at Griff Farm, near Helmsley, where the Duncombe Park oxen were kept. The equivalent of the horseman was the ox man. Usually after two years' work oxen were fattened, killed and salted for hung beef for winter.

The three ox bow stones—one formerly at the head of Farndale, a second at Ash House, Farndale, and a third at Underpark, Eskdale—are as far as we know unique in the British Isles (*see plate* 41). It is surmised that hazel sticks, held in position by pegs placed in the holes in their bases, were bent round them to make bows for ox yokes. Also a stone with a round hole through it, about six feet off the ground, projecting from the gable end of Duck House, Farndale, is said to have been used for the making of withies—ropes of willow.[1] The method has not been remembered. It was usual to secure the bow which passed through holes in the yoke by a wooden peg, but the oxen kept up to about 1900 on the Duncombe Park estate have the bows fastened to the yoke by twisted withies (*see plate* 43).

In this century the improvement of cattle was encouraged by the formation of agricultural societies and shows and also by the progeny of the Feversham herd of shorthorns at Duncombe Park, Helmsley, itself descended from Bates of Kirkleavington stock. Well-known breeders were J. W. Harrison of Underpark, Eskdale, known as 'Shorthorn Johnnie', the Wainds of Ankness, Bransdale, and at the present day the Listers of Browside, Glaisdale.

At the other end of the scale were the many cowkeepers, often the craftsmen, keeping one or two cows, occupying a cowkeeping place with a grass field or two, and either selling milk locally or making butter. Some of these, who had no land, rented cow gates on the verges of the lanes set out in the enclosure awards. Here old men or old women acting as cow-tenters looked after them. For instance at Pickering twenty-five cows grazed on one side of the beck and twenty

[1] Mr Amos Brecon, who formerly lived at Duck House.

on the other, whilst at Helmsley about ninety cows belonging to some fifty cow-keepers used to be pastured in a large field called Beckdale. The practice ceased about the end of the First World War.

That horses were sent from this area to London for the King's use in the fourteenth century, and for that matter for the Queen's use in the twentieth, confirms Marshall's truism that 'Yorkshire has long been famous for its horses'. He estimated that in a year 'five to ten thousand were bred between the Eastern Moorlands and the Humber'.

'In Cleveland and the Dales you rarely saw any real Cart Horses ... [They were] all bays with black legs', wrote Lumley Hodgson of the first half of the last century.[1] He was describing a type of horse specific to Cleveland and the moorland dales, what is now called the Cleveland Bay, a pure ancient breed, formerly in general use on the farm, but developed as a coach horse—hence its place in the Royal Mews at the present day. A few breeders in or near the dales and elsewhere keep these now comparatively rare but highly prized horses (*see plate* 255).

Within recollection the horses kept for farm work were the Clydesdale and the Shire, or a cross between the two. Many were cross-breds: 'Farmers liked a bit o' blood, so that they could hunt 'em.' Or a cross between a Clydesdale and a good galloway made a trap horse that could take half a plough. The number kept naturally depended on the size of the farm. On a sixty-acre dales' holding they might have eleven—five for work, two foals, two two-year-olds and the mares.

Broken in at two years old and worked for two years, they were then sold as five-year-olds for from £20 to £50. On a farm of over 100 acres the sale of young horses in the spring and backend was counted on to pay the rent. Agents used to tour the farms to buy colts for the mines, railways and breweries, and stock was also taken to sell at Yarm and Egton Fairs.

Daily grooming, breaking in, staying up overnight to attend births and four feeds a day were part of the routine of a farm. The horses were fed at 5.30 a.m. They returned from the fields at dinner time, and afterwards a second pair was brought out. By the time they had been stabled and fed, the harness cleaned and other stock attended to, it might be 8 p.m. Then all the horsemen round about met at a stable and played cards or merrills on the corn bin lid by candlelight until 9 p.m., by which time the young men had to return indoors (*see plate* 264).

Whenever and for whatever purposes the horses were taken on main roads or

---

[1] Letters written by Lumley Hodgson, 1883, recalling fifty years earlier, *Cleveland Bay Magazine*, 1968. See also Sir Alfred Pease, 'The Cleveland Bay and the Yorkshire Coach Horse', *Transactions of the Yorkshire Agricultural Society*, no. 94, 1936. J. Fairfax-Blakeborough, *The Cleveland Bay*; and the present authors' *The Wonders of Yorkshire*, 1959.

into towns their tails were plaited and sometimes bobbed, that is rolled up, fastened with a band with the plait showing in the centre. Also 'a decent farm could always fit up three or four sets of brasses at the least'. For shows Cleveland Bays traditionally have their manes tied up in little plaits fastened off with horse hair, and the harness of cart horses is adorned with braid and brasses, plus in the last twenty years wax and paper flowers (*see plate* 254). Harness was oiled four times a year, and the sale of horse hair to local dealers was a 'perk' for the farm boys.

Fairs for the sale of horses, to a lesser extent cattle, and in later days sheep used to be held on certain Tuesdays throughout the year at Egton until the start of Ruswarp mart. Groups of 'into teens' of farmers drove animals to it, and dealers coming from far afield led them away in bunches tied halter to halter and tail to tail. One of the stopping places on the way to York was Hamer House, the inn called the Lettered Board, on Rosedale Moor. Dealers were always said to 'put a glass of rum in their boots'.[1] Started in 1889, Egton Show has developed from the fairs.

In general two types of sheep are to be found in the area—the inside sheep which nowadays means Leicesters, Mashams, Suffolks and Oxfords, and the moor sheep, the Blackface and the Swaledale. The latter, now outnumbering the Blackface, were introduced by James Calvert of Keld, Swaledale, who moved with some of his flock to near Langdale End, Hackness, in 1921, and also by Estill Peacock who, a year later buying an aged Swaledale ram and two lambs from James Hodgson of Askrigg, Wensleydale, took them to North Ghyll, Farndale.

Nowhere enclosed, the heather-clad moorlands have sustained the many small flocks of Blackface sheep since time immemorial.[2] They were once the most numerous breed in the British Isles, and are still the main type kept on the Scottish moors. Well-known breeders, such as Willie Smith of Hunt House, Goathland, Mr A. Agar of Egton and Mr F. Boocock, who farmed at Moorsholm for forty-three years, used to go annually to buy rams in Scotland and Northumberland. Formerly, says Mr H. Peirson of Hartoft, these sheep had heavier longer coats, shorter legs and blacker faces, but the Scottish rams have been crossed with the Swaledale to give a finer coat. Blackface wool is none the less more valuable than Swaledale. Both breeds are 'heeafed'—that is, the flocks know and stay on their own territory. Some lamb on the open moor—'A very *fendable* thing is a moor lamb'.

[1] Recollections of Mr G. S. Hutton, Sneaton, Mr T. Eddon, born at Hamer, and Mr. A. Agar of Egton.
[2] B. Waites, *Moorland and Valeland Farming in North-East Yorkshire*, 1967, Borthwick Papers no. 32, pp. 26–33.

Because of the vast extent of the moors sheep stealing has been endemic. In the seventeenth century it occurs time and again in Quarter Sessions records, and when in 1820 a Blackface sheep breeders' association was formed, it was called the 'Goathland, Saltersgate and Levisham Association for prosecuting felons'. Even in 1924 the association offered £5 for information leading to conviction, and the Sheep Keepers' Guide, containing all the marks and owners, has been published from time to time, partly to keep a check on charges of sheep stealing (*see page* 27).

Other difficulties have beset the sheep men. The unenclosed moors have not until very recently, and then only in certain parts, been stinted: that is, a specific number of sheep to be allowed on the moor allotted to each farm, so that over-stocking and disputes over boundaries have abounded. One concerned with trespassing in Bilsdale came into the courts in 1970. On that account some farmers have preferred not to keep sheep. Besides this the spread of bracken and the vast acreage taken over by the Forestry Commission have drastically reduced the extent of sheep strays, and as if that were not enough, sheep are killed by motor vehicles on the open moorland roads. These factors, together with the considerable work involved with a small flock, have reduced the total number kept. On the other hand a few men have very large flocks—into thousands.

In the old days sheep used to be carefully nurtured. There was generally a sheep field of old sward on a farm, and a meadow with plenty of rib grass and yellow rattle which they liked kept for sheep hay. Mr Jim Ainsley recalls that in the winter of 1917 when he was living at Spout House, Bilsdale, he had some Scotch sheep up Spout Bank, and late one afternoon he found them playing and jumping about—a sure sign of a storm to come. The snow lasted for thirteen weeks, and during that time he daily carried as much hay as he could with a doubled plough cord, knocked down branches, and felled *hollins* (holly trees) for them to eat the bark. Then one day when he arrived as usual, there were no sheep. They knew. The storm was over and he had to take back his bundle of hay.

Salving is not remembered.[1] Mr F. Dowson, Rosedale, tells us that his father used to salve, but he also designed the first walk-out tub for dipping in the dale in 1884 (*see plate* 49). Washing sheep, undertaken often by daytal men for perhaps 2s. 6d. a day and a bottle of gin, was an annual but not a social event (*see plate* 52).

On the other hand the great gatherings for clipping were looked forward to from year to year. Forty-four men are remembered sitting down to a meal at High Row Mires, Hartoft. 'Nearly a feast' was put on beginning at ten o'clock, with

[1] For salving see Marie Hartley and Joan Ingilby, *Life and Tradition in the Yorkshire Dales*, 1968, pp. 42–4.

special clipping-day cheesecakes cooked with butter spread on them, for dinner a hot roast and baked suet pudding followed by plum pudding with rum sauce, and later a cold supper included pease pudding made from soaked dried peas boiled with herbs.

A whole week early in July was spent going on from one clipping day to another, and this still continues on a few farms, for instance at Hunt House, Elm House, Farndale and Red House, Hackness (*see also plate* 54). Unlike in the Pennine dales the work is undertaken indoors, and most men, some now using

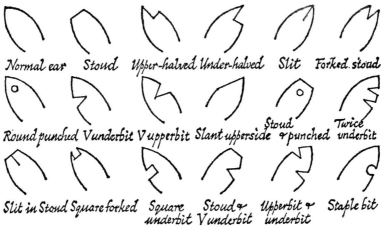

SHEEP EAR MARKS

electric shears, clip standing up, then kneeling, whilst others, usually the older men, clip the sheep on raised benches on which one knee or foot may be rested. Sometimes the fleeces are laid out flat and left to roll up later. When about 500 sheep are waiting there is no time to waste.

Sheep sales mark the culmination of the year's work (*see plate* 60). On those days the moorland roads for miles around used to be filled with sheep, and everyone came to visit relations and friends. Mr F. W. Nesfield (b. 1881) remembers his father describing the Goathland sale held in the open near the Cross Pipes inn (near the church). There were no pens and the flocks were kept separate by the dogs. Afterwards every room in the inn was converted into a bar and drinking and singing went on until 3 a.m. Once riding home from the sale an elderly farmer and two lads were caught in a fog over the moor. The farmer's pony was given its head and after a long time it suddenly stopped. The rider put out his stick, and feeling something hard, exclaimed 'Whya, it's oor gate.'

Last, but not by any means the least important in farm economy, is the pig. Pig-keeping had continued from the Middle Ages when swine fed on mast in the forests. In more recent times the conditions—of hundreds of small farms growing potatoes and barley—were favourable for the rearing of pigs. Bacon was an all important item of diet in the home, and bacon and hams were exported.

During the last 150 years the farms in the moorland valleys, the Vale of Pickering and to a lesser extent the Wolds were largely the suppliers of the famous York ham. Marshall tells us that about 1750 a new breed of pig, a mixed 'black-sandy' Berkshire, had been introduced, and that it was 'fatted, butchered and sold to bacon-makers who salt and dry them for the London and West Yorkshire markets'.

The breed now remembered, superseded today by the Large White, is known by various names, some of them being: the 'Blue and White', the 'Blood Breed' or the 'Bilsdale Blue'. Distinguished by blue blotches on the skin, they made good mothers, fattened quickly and ate anything, even docks. But in turn, when the taste for lean meat began about 1924, they went out of fashion.

Farmers kept from a dozen to two dozen pigs. Stone washing troughs for potatoes and set pots in which they were boiled in nets, and pig creels and scalding tubs (*see drawings on page* 111) for use when pigs were slaughtered were part of the general equipment. In some villages the two latter were kept communally and a fee paid for their use. Flailing and grinding were made tediously lengthy because of the need for barley meal for pigs. Pig-killing days were occasions for parties, and hams were often hung all over the rafters of granaries. Cottagers usually sold a ham to pay for the next young pig, and they vied with one another as to who had the heaviest when slaughtered—perhaps a carcase of fifty-seven stones.

The export trade was run by private enterprise. Joseph Ford records that in the first half of the nineteenth century, reaching a climax about 1860, vast quantities of bacon were cured by two brothers named Smith at the Fat Ox, Houlsyke, Eskdale. There were a bacon curing warehouse in the old paper mill at Lealholm in 1860, and a large business in hams, packed in hogsheads, sent from Pickering to London in the latter part of the last century. Many butchers combined a bacon curing business with their normal trade. But this mostly ceased in 1924 when the Bacon Marketing Board was formed and a licence to kill pigs and cure bacon became compulsory; and by the Second World War the mild Danish method of wet rather than dry curing had become popular.

Two families, the Simpsons of Gillamoor and the Harts of Ugthorpe, take up the thread of the story to the present day. The Simpsons' firm was established in 1830, and won a prize in London in 1887 for 'matured Pale Dried Hams'. In the middle of the last century George Simpson combined the selling of provender, maize and cattle cake with the purchase of pigs, eggs and butter. Starting about 4 a.m. he travelled once a week to York, baiting at Hovingham, to deliver goods to shops there. The next generation, Hawson and George, kept many pigs and bought others 'off the *cammeril*'—that is, without the offal and off the wooden bar on which slaughtered pigs were hung.

At Gillamoor they still have the salt house for drysalting, and the smoke house, a two-storied building with an iron door on the ground floor and an iron grille forming an upper floor under which a turf fire covered with a bucket of oak sawdust smouldered. Wetted and covered with pea flour, which absorbed the smoke, about a hundred hams left in for a few days could be hung and smoked in the upper story.

Every season they sent 6,000 hams packed in tierces by rail to the Army and Navy Stores in London, and all the year round hams were despatched to Harrods. Nearer at hand, old established factors and grocers at York, hotels and distinguished private customers were supplied.

The firm of Harts was founded about 1864 by Dinnis Hart (1842–1930) son of Francis the village blacksmith, aided by his wife Alice, who lived to be 104. Buying pigs locally, they killed them and dry-cured hams and bacon in winter, hanging them in two thatched cottages where the temperature was ideal. The Harts went weekly to Whitby market for forty-one years, Dinnis with sucking pigs and Alice with bacon. Their son and grandson, both called Aaron Hart, followed on.

Hams, sewn in hessian, were sent by rail all over England and Scotland. Sometimes sixty at a time went to Cornwall, and formerly they despatched up to 300 each spring to Rowntrees at Scarborough. But increases in rail charges made sending long distances uneconomical. The factory at Ugthorpe, supplying wholesalers, still continues on a large scale, and as a sideline they also make curd for cheesecakes—one of the still continuing delicacies of Yorkshire.

CATTLE

42. *Mr John Potter Waind (1878–1934), well-known breeder of Shorthorn cattle, Mr S. Waind and Mr John Waind (1828–1901) with the stock bull on the right and other beasts at Ankness Farm, Bransdale (before 1900).*

43. *Oxen and cart at Helmsley. The oxen were used up to a late date on the Duncombe Park estate. They were stabled at the home farm, Griff Farm, near Helmsley. The bows were held in place by twisted withies; the animals' nose-rings were joined by a chain and they were attached to the cart-pole by the ring on the yoke (c. 1900).*

MILK

44. *Mr J. W. Morley on Darkie taking milk by sledge to the main road from Ramsdale Farm, Fylingthorpe* (c. 1957).

45. *Mrs Mary Peason, who was born at High Thorn, Esklets, Westerdale. She married and came to Hole House, Fryup. Afflicted with rheumatism, she dragged herself up after milking by the tail of the cow, which was used to it* (c. 1890).

SHEEP AND LAMBS

46. *Mr J. Atkinson, High Row Mires, Hartoft, sends sheep and lambs back to the moor after marking the lambs at Low Hamer.*

47. *Mr H. Atkinson of Goathland House holds a late lamb when gathering sheep for clipping on Goathland Moor (1971).*

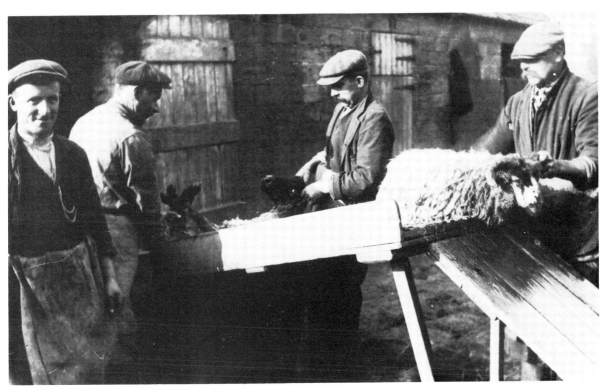

49. *Sheep dipping at Duck House, Farndale* (c. *1907*).

48. *Mr J. Atkinson marking a lamb.
His mark is slit near ear and upper
bit far ear.*

50. *Pet lambs. Either Farndale or Rosedale. Note turf stack on
left* (c. *1908*).

SHEEP WASHING

51. *Sheep being driven into pens by Mr Frank Morley and his sons of St Ives Farm, Fylingdales, preparatory to washing near the head-waters of the River Derwent where Fylingdales Moor joins Wykeham Moors below Lilla Howe* (c. 1910).

52. *Sheep washing in progress. John, Frank and Peter Morley are standing in the water, whilst their father looks on. John Harland holds a sheep. The pool and pen were completely washed out in a cloudburst in the 1930s* (c. 1910).

SHEEP CLIPPING

53. *A group assembled at a sheep clipping day at John Peirson's, Thornhill Farm, Goathland, June 1898. It was usual to come in best clothes, and to wear blue overalls, hence the light-coloured washed out garments. The barn in the background was formerly the thatched cruck-built farmhouse dating from 1699.*

54. *Clipping day at Mr H. Atkinson's, Goathland House, Goathland. Some men are clipping by hand, some by machine, and two in the foreground are wrapping (1967).*

△

55–8. *Mr Geoffrey Feather-stone clips a Blackface ewe at Hutton-le-Hole.*

59. *Miss Rose Farrow, who shepherds the flock that grazes the green at Hutton-le-Hole, wraps fleeces.*

SHEEP CLIPPING

SALES

60. *The eleventh annual show and sale of 1,977 moor and half-bred sheep at Blakey between Hutton-le-Hole and Castleton. Boulton and Cooper are the auctioneers here and at Goathland. The Lion Inn is in the background (1970).*

61. *Sale at Lumley House Farm, Danbydale.*

SHEEP DOGS

62 Mr M. W. Cook, Park Farm, Kildale. A well-known contestant in sheep dog trials with Tip and Maid.

63. Mr J. W. Mackley, Low Horcum, gathering sheep near Saltersgate in the early morning (1930s).

▽

64. *Johnnie Stroud, Thorgill, Rosedale, who rode about his donkey selling kippers, bloaters and oranges (c. 1900).*

65. *Granpa Leadley of Sproxton on 'The Ass' always so-called. In the background is the N.E.R. omnibus which took people to Gilling to catch the train for York (c. 1865).*

DONKEYS

66. *Low Hawsker? c. 1902. Donkeys carried cans of milk into Whitby.*

67. *Mr W. Champion, Westfield Grange, near Cropton, feeds a litter of pigs. Round troughs, formerly of stone and later of iron, were usual (c. 1938).*

69. *Mr Willie Smith (1821–1914), Hunt House, Goathland, a noted breeder of Black-face sheep, here brings food to a sow, one of the old breed of pigs kept in the moorland dales (c. 1911).*

68. *Mr G. H. Simpson, Gillamoor, salting hams and bacon.*

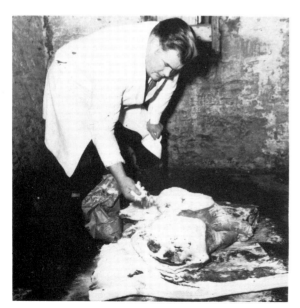

CARTER'S NEWLY-INVENTED THRASHING MACHINES.

FOUNDRIES

70. *Woodcut accompanying Christopher Carter's (Rhydale Foundry, Kirkbymoorside) advertisement in the* Malton Messenger *of 27th May 1856. Described as a portable thrashing machine, it was made for from two to five horses. Improvements to it were advertised in the following year. The horse is being driven in a clockwise direction, but the woodcut may not have been reversed.*

71. *Albert Foundry, Pickering. Mr Frank Dobson, Mr George Pennock and Mr Jack Dobson tapping the furnace before pouring molten metal into the moulds for casting (*c. *1900).*

THE IMPLEMENT MAKERS

IN the first half of the nineteenth century, following the Industrial Revolution, the many journeymen on the move encouraged the opening of local foundries for the making of agricultural implements. Several serving the area of our survey were established. At the same time many of the early English makers—Samuelson of Banbury, Kearsley of Ripon, Howard of Bedford, Burgess and Key of Essex, Bamlett of Thirsk, and Ransomes, Sims and Jefferies of Ipswich—were exhibiting at local shows, advertising in local papers and employing local agents. In spite of competition the foundries and implement makers of the region succeeded, and although most sooner or later came to an end and only a very few still continue, they made an outstanding contribution to this era of invention.

The availability of natural resources played a part and had a long tradition. Bloomeries for smelting iron and right of ploughbote (wood for ploughs) date back to the Middle Ages. In the nineteenth century suitable timber, pig-iron from ironstone mined in nearby hills and smelted at Middlesbrough, and a supply of the different sands required for casting were at hand.

All the foundries started to make and improve on the small horse-drawn implements then in use, such as wood and iron ploughs, plain rollers and harrows. At that time the only means of power was the horse wheel, which was able to drive light machinery such as small threshers, chaff and turnip cutters, oil cake breakers and, although almost too much for the horses, grinding mills (*see plate* 122). But soon steam engines, drills, mowers and reapers were to appear. It was a challenging time. 'People had to think for themselves. New ideas were coming up, and they had to grasp them', Mr J. W. Carter said to us.

In the following decades local agricultural implement makers were too numerous to mention individually; not all ran foundries and many combined their function with that of millwright. Chapman's at Whitby and Isaac Hartas at the Wrelton Works, already mentioned, existed in the 1840s and were as far as we know the earliest. The latter, besides kitchen ranges, turned out ploughs, turnip cutters and horse wheels and barn threshers.

At Pickering in the 1850s and 1860s there were Sootheran and Carr, brass- and iron-founders, Fletcher Bros., who made kitchen ranges, also John Weighell, one of the most interesting, who opened the Albert Foundry. Weighell's made the machines already mentioned, also grass mowers, reaping machines at £15 apiece and grinding mills (*see plate* 122).[1] In 1879 the Albert Foundry, which had ceased to run, was restarted by Francis Dobson, who had been a blacksmith at Wrelton (*see plate* 71). Making ranges for farmhouses, frying pans, plough shares, implements and specializing in boring and fixing pumps, the foundry continued until the death of Jack Dobson, Francis's nephew, in 1960.

At Kirkbymoorside there were again several makers, of whom the Carters and the Russells are the most important. In his lifetime, Mr J. W. Carter gave us the following information about his family. It is thought that the Carters came here from Ponteland near Newcastle at the time of the '45 Rebellion, and in the early nineteenth century Thomas Carter, blacksmith at Kirkbymoorside, had four sons: Christopher, Joseph, Thomas and Henry.

In the 1840s Christopher, the eldest son and the most inventive, started the Ryedale Foundry, next to the present Kirk Forge, and he made the usual implements including his newly-invented portable threshing machine (*see plate* 70). Christopher manufactured bricks and tiles, supplied Kirkbymoorside and Robin Hood's Bay with gas, and laid the first piped water supply to the former. He also won a match of 'Knor and Spell' played on Shrove Tuesday, 1857. But aged forty-nine he died, and in 1870 the foundry and stock were sold.

Meanwhile in the 1850s his brother Joseph, a blacksmith, helped by the bachelor brother, Thomas, started a small foundry. Joseph went to London to see the underground railways being built, watched a steam engine pumping water, carried the idea in his head, and when he returned home he made a beam engine. Developing this line, he advertised 'Steam engines and hydraulic engines of every description from a Hand Pump to a Bramah's High Pressure', also ovens, ranges, stoves and boilers. The foundry was carried on by his son Thomas until 1898.

The youngest brother, Henry, began his career at Darlington working on the 'Derwent' engine built by Alfred Kitching in 1845, now to be seen at Darlington station, and when there he was offered employment as engineer to the cloth manufacturer, later Sir Titus Salt. However, he set up the Cyclops Foundry in Tinley Garth, Kirkbymoorside, carried on by his sons and grandson, J. W. Carter, until 1953.

Here, they used No. 1 Scotch pig-iron sent by rail and fetched from Gilling station by horse and waggon; they burnt foundry coke from the Weardale and

[1] *Malton Messenger*, 22nd January 1859; 1st April 1854; 4th August 1855; 8th August 1863.

later the Consett Iron Companies, and used two types of sand, one for moulds from Rudland Moor and the other for cores from Yoadwath Common. There was a continual demand for castings for agricultural implements. Patterns fashioned in red deal for the moulds were kept for every contingency. 'They made anything in cast iron—implements of all kinds, wheels for hen houses and sheep racks to ones four to five feet in diameter for water carts, also tanks, Cambridge rollers, water wheel castings, of which the largest remembered, a boss, weighed seven hundred-weight, and the famous Carter ovens and ranges. They never turned a job away.'

It was hard work, much of it undertaken kneeling down; and they wore 'common shoes' as the soles cracked, and had to be replaced. The casting of *socks* (shares), sold at 9*d.* or even 8*d.* each, was 'slavery'. In the end the coming of the farm tractor, together with electric welding and other modern inventions were the cause of the closing down. Some of the patterns and castings may be seen at the Ryedale Folk Museum.

'Ploughs', says George Russell, 'are designed for a locality', and this assertion is well illustrated here. Iron and wood, swing and wheel ploughs were made by local blacksmiths and joiners. There were for instance Aaron Willis of Wombleton, who won many prizes for his ploughs in the 1850s, and Jack Linton of Ugthorpe remembered as famous for Linton ploughs forged with a striking hammer. The two best-known, however, were the John Wood of Bilsdale and the North Cave, the one popular in Ryedale and the other in Eskdale.

In the 1840s William Wood, a miller, and his family, moved from Howl Cauldron Mill, Kirkdale, to Fangdale Beck, a hamlet in Bilsdale. When one of the sons, John (1855–1937), was seventeen he quarrelled with his father and went to Manchester, where he learnt of new uses for water power. Returning to Fang-dale Beck, he constructed a small overshot as opposed to the more usual under-shot wheel,[1] and later invented the gearing for a pony to supplement this when water failed. Provided with power and with the help of journeymen requiring a few weeks' work, he started up a foundry, making his first cast-iron plough in 1874. Later he visited Sheffield to seek advice on the casting of shares and learnt the method of chilling by piping water to the bottom of a casting to harden the base.

It is remembered that about 1900, on the left of the blacksmith's shop, which together with the water wheel is still there, stood a ten-foot-high furnace, heated with coke, for smelting pig-iron sent from Middlesbrough and fetched from Ingleby Greenhow station eight miles away. In the shop were three forges, and,

[1] J. W. Carter, 'Wheels Recall the Skill of Country Craftsmen', *The Dalesman*, vol. XXIII, 1961, p. 572.

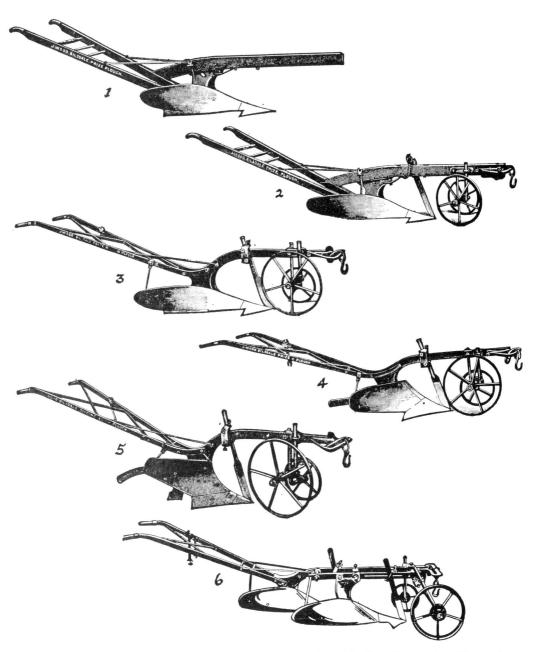

JOHN WOOD OR BILSDALE PLOUGHS *from the original wood-engravings illustrating a small undated catalogue issued from Driffield probably a few years after they moved there in 1911. 1 Dales' plough—a wooden plough for thin ploughing marked W E. 2 Wooden plough for light or medium soils marked HWL. 3 Plough for strong land marked HWN; price £8 10s. 4 Light digging plough marked W F; price £7 12s. 6d. 5 Digging plough marked W N. 6 Double furrow plough price £11 15s.*

all run by water power, a home-made drilling machine, a lathe, a grindstone, a fan for blowing the furnace and (used once a week) a butter churn yoked by a belt. At that time four men and two apprentices working from 7 a.m. to 7 p.m. were paid respectively 18s. and 1s. a week.[1]

In John Ainsley's time there were three moulders, two blacksmiths, and four casuals or daytal men, local men who went once a week on casting day. 'In hot weather it was murder.' Two men carried a ladle containing ten stones of red-hot metal from the furnace several yards to the sand house, where the moulders had prepared the boxes by pressing patterns in sand. A ladleful filled two dozen boxes making a plough share, pig trough or other objects.

In 1915 the daytal men went on strike for almost three months for 6d. a day extra—2s. 6d. instead of 2s. Wood gave it to them, but reorganized the system so that they worked half an hour longer and produced eighteen more shares. Nevertheless his men speak of him as a good master who never passed shoddy work.

Every part of a plough except the bolts was made, and using assembly line methods a plough was turned out in a day. In early times one cost £2 10s. It was usual here as elsewhere to make ploughs with modifications for different types of land and to distinguish them by initials cast in raised letters on the mouldboard. They were taken from the names of Bilsdale men: W A (William Ainsley) denoted one with a disc-coulter for prize ploughing; W N (William Noble) was a digging plough; and W B (William Barr) was a light strong plough for thin ploughing. H was added to these initials for heavier types. The lightest weighed ten stones and the heaviest nineteen and a half[2] (*see page* 33).

A load of ploughs used to be taken to Helmsley market every Friday. Mr J. Bentley, Old Byland Grange, tells us: 'Mi Dad used to say that John Wood came to Rievaulx Bank Top [a junction with the Helmsley–Bilsdale road] and he met him there and brought back a plough on a cart. It cost £3. This was over fifty years ago. It was easy to pull, easy draught, easy to steer—you could plough 'em wi' one hand. They allus ploughed even. The best single furrow for our land.'

Thinking of moving nearer to a railway, John Wood built a house in Kirkbymoorside, but in 1911 a business came up for sale in Driffield and he started the Bilsdale Plough Company there run by his two sons, and he himself continued to live at Fangdale Beck until 1925.

Wood was tall and muscular, and many tales are handed down of his prowess in

[1] Recollections of Mr J. W. Carter, who was head moulder here in the early twentieth century; also Mr John Ainsley, Bilsdale, who worked here, and Mr Jim Ainsley.
[2] Catalogue of Bilsdale ploughs issued from Driffield about 1920, lent by Mr W. Wheldon and Mr L. Atkinson, John Wood's grandsons.

foot-races and cricket. He forged his wife's wedding ring from a gold sovereign and, a touch added for good measure, it is said in competition with Tommy Ransome (the implement maker), whose gold turned to dust. It is true that Wood was often heard to say that Ransome was his only rival.

On the other side of the moorlands the North Cave plough was being made at a works at Ruswarp and by joiners in other villages round Whitby. It originated in the village of North Cave near Hull, where William Saunders, who made ploughs, flourished as a blacksmith in the 1840s, and whose son, Richard Saunders (1811–1894), is described as 'Plough Maker formerly of North Cave' on his tombstone in Tickton churchyard near Beverley. Richard established a small foundry eventually run by Saunders and Hicks, and now still owned by Mr T. E. Hicks, who remembers castings being sent far afield, for instance to the Watsons, joiners of Sneaton, near Whitby, who made these ploughs up to about 1950.

The story of how the plough came into that district has been told us by Mr E. Benson of Ruswarp. In the 1850s his great-grandfather, a farmer of Cross Butts, near Whitby, went to judge a ploughing competition at North Cave. The prize was a plough which he bought from the winner, and bringing it back he eventually took it to pieces with a view to making others like it.

In 1869 Henry Benson, son of the farmer, started up a works as millwright and ploughmaker near the present iron bridge at Ruswarp. They felled suitably shaped trees in the woods for handles, 7 feet 2 inches long, and for the beams, 6 feet 6 inches long, forged the ordinary ironwork but had castings from templates taken from the original plough made at Batt's Foundry, Whitby, at Weighell's at Pickering, or at Tinsley's foundry at Loftus. A stamp bearing the inscription 'Henry Benson' was sent to the foundries, and was pressed into the sand at the bottom of the boxes for making mouldboards which in this way had the name imprinted on them. They had their own design for wooden *stowers*, the top turned wooden stay between the handles.

Ploughs were made different heights to suit the size of a man. The plough was turned upside down, and the distance between the ground and the handles was measured with a stick kept for the purpose. They were given three coats of red lead paint; the ironwork was blackened, and they were mostly sold up the dales as far as Westerdale. A wheel plough cost £2 15s. and a swing £1 15s., but towards the end farmers brought in the old ironwork for re-use. The firm finished at the beginning of the last war, by which time Ransome's, who had been making the shares, had ceased to do so.

A firm whose work spread into the dales was that of Ralph Yates, the Derwent Foundry, Malton. This started in a small way in 1845, but keeping up with the times and taking on agencies they became a large concern, still flourishing. Makers of horse wheels, they bought up the patterns of these when the Wrelton Works closed, and they were pioneers of the threshing contracting business with sets of steam engines and threshing machines touring the district (*see plates* 130–3). This business, says Mr R. Yates, never paid anyone, but it kept firms in touch with their clients, a valuable asset in days of barter—of exchanging wool or stock for implements or threshing.

Mr Ralph Yates (b. 1895) grandson of the founder, tells a story of his uncle, Alfred, then in his teens. In 1888 he was helping to assemble a Bamlett mower, when an old gentleman came into the yard and asked what the machine was. Alfred promptly replied, 'It's a Bamlett, sir, the very best in the world', to which the old man answered, 'Good boy. I'm Mr Bamlett of Thirsk, the maker of the mower', and gave him a gold sovereign.

As the Malton agent for Massey Harris of Canada Yates sold 200 self-binders between 1890 and 1894. They were shipped to Liverpool where the Massey Harris men erected them, and sent by rail, with as many as twenty-eight in a load, to Malton where they were completed. It has to be remembered that these large farms were a little ahead of the moorland dales' farms where self-binders only became general by the end of the First World War.

The Russells of Kirkbymoorside, now a firm employing over eighty men, started from similar beginnings as the rest. Early in the last century they were blacksmiths and innkeepers at the Griffin Inn on the Thirsk–Easingwold road, and one of them, setting out as they did in those days with a bag of tools over his shoulder, found work with a smith at Salton, four miles south of Kirkbymoorside. He eventually started up on his own at Great Edstone near by, and in 1855 won a prize for the best assortment of forged iron ploughs at the Ryedale Show.

His son, George Fletcher Russell, settling at Kirkbymoorside as a blacksmith, invented a turnip drill combined with a fertilizer, whose special feature was a glass bottom on which the fertilizer, always sticky, would not cling. The story goes that it was taken to Driffield market where, with sand substituted for fertilizer, it was shown off in the street. G. F. Russell used to journey round to farms and, provided with wood by the farmer, make drills at the blacksmiths' shops. His drills were also sent to Russia and exhibited at the Smithfield Show.

The firm, the Yorkshire Patent Manure Drill and Agricultural Implement Co. Ltd. went into liquidation, but about 1909, strengthened by members of the next generation, started up again as T. B. Russell. In those days they were only local suppliers, serving an area within walking or cycling distance, and they did not have a foundry.

Mr George Russell, connected with the firm since he was a boy of thirteen and managing director for twenty years, remembers going on foot with his grandfather (G. F. Russell) to Farndale, and staying two or three nights to repair barn threshing machines and horse wheels. He also worked on the wheels and turbines of the many local corn mills. Using hornbeam and crab for the cogging, he himself built the machinery of Bransdale mill, and taking his own *mill bills* (picks and chisels), dressed the millstones. Hornbeam and crab were bought in and seasoned for years.

The firm made traps, waggons at £25, and pioneered the use of rubber tyres on carts for which axle, wheels and India tyres cost £9. In the bad times of 1928, when the work force fell to five men, George Russell took these carts to sell for £26 apiece at Stokesley market.

They repaired steam engines and threshing machines, and sold and serviced dairy equipment. When self-binders came in, they sold the various makes, perhaps one a year, including the cheapest made by Hornsby of Grantham at £18 each. As still is the case, farmers could not afford many new goods, but bought them at farm sales. In those days machines were brought to the works for repair, whereas today the firm's mechanics go to the farms.

Machines for seeding, and allied implements such as gappers for singling turnips, have always been the Russells' prime interest. Mr George Russell himself has taken out twenty-four patents. Besides acting as agents and selling combine harvesters, they make, amongst other implements, hand seeders, different drills for horticultural purposes, harrows, elevators and harvesters. Today their machines are sent to the Sudan, the Congo, and other parts of the world.

LIFE IN THE VALLEYS

UP to fifty or sixty years ago the people of the moorland valleys enjoyed a degree of self-sufficiency that had gone earlier from other districts. It was achieved by a prodigality of labour and effort soon to become neither acceptable nor available. 'Time was cheap.' Monetary reward was not the criterion; barter was common, and little money circulated. The thatches of dwellings in the old days served as hiding-places for gold sovereigns. 'Their money bags in the thatch/Was hid with careful thought', wrote Thomas Parker, thatcher and poet of Wombleton.

Neighbourliness evinced itself in the many communal activities. Over a hundred years ago there were flailing and stone-rearing or *grovven* days, the latter to clear the fields and build walls,[1] and up to the 1940s ploughing, flitting, threshing, and clipping days, of which the last two continue here and there in a minor way. It was customary to help in an emergency with the loan of labour, a horse or an implement. 'If one was poorly, they were all poorly', was said of Farndale. The poor were assisted with gifts of fruit, fry at a pig killing, with cheap milk, or the loan of a strip of land for growing potatoes.

The simple pleasures of ring games, parties at Christmas, at pig killings and bee takings, chapel anniversaries, a trip to Whitby or Sunday School outings to Scarborough were looked forward to from year to year. In the autumn and winter the different hunts provided sport. Older people recollecting this close-knit inter-related community with few strangers, especially in the small dales off Eskdale, dwell with nostalgia on the happiness of the days of fifty or even twenty years ago.

Foremost amongst the factors breaking up the old way of life were the gradual introduction of machinery involving more capital expenditure, the replacement of horses by tractors in the 1940s and 1950s, and in consequence of both these a reduced labour force lessening the number of people living on each farm. In the first quarter of this century on a 180-acre farm 't' maister' or 't' boss', a foreman, horseman, and lad were usual, and on a 100-acre farm two useful youths besides

---

[1] See also pp. 66 et seq.; Joseph Ford, *Some Reminiscences and Folk Lore of Danby Parish and District*, 1953, pp. 29, 137–9; and Mr Linley, Stonebank, Rosedale, who remembers George Smith of Hartoft speaking of *grovven* days.

the master. Even this was less than the comparative number of a hundred years ago.

In those days it was possible for a man and his wife to start on a smallholding of 'teens of acres' with £20 as capital, and if they began on a sixty-acre farm with £200 they were considered fairly well off. In the last century a man could manage with a plough, a pair of wooden harrows, a sledge and a pair of galloways.[1] Up to the First World War a cart, a waggon, a plough, a set of harrows, a grass cutter and a reaper borrowed on occasion sufficed.[2] Or the following served many a man into the 1920s: one or two ploughs, blacksmith-made harrows, a scrubber (clod-crusher), a scruffler (rubbish clearer), a Cambridge roller, a put-off reaper, a horse wheel and barn threshing machine, and a dog cart or trap and a waggon or two.[3]

Many people have described to us their experiences on smallholdings. 'We were made for work—donkey fashion.' On small and medium sized farms 'you didn't expect to make money. If you had one more calf than the year before you were satisfied'. Several acres of oats provided fodder for horses and cattle; a strip of barley was grown for meal for pigs and a few acres of potatoes, turnips and cabbages supplied vegetables for consumption by man and beast. From time to time a sheep was killed and the mutton shared with a neighbour. The women sold butter and eggs (once at 8d. a pound and 10d. a score) which 'brought back' the groceries. Many who kept bees had honey for sale, and all having poultry sold cock chickens and geese fed on the stubble for Christmas. The dictum was, 'If you have a bit of everything you're all right.'

When he was a boy some seventy years ago Mr Fred Handley lived in Farndale and used to walk to Rosedale Abbey for yeast. The shopkeeper made up a pound into sixteen packets sold at 1d. each. Then his mother sold them in Farndale at ½d. more, making 8d. profit on the transaction.

The growing of a few acres of wheat to be ground for meal for flour at a local mill, the acme of self sufficiency, was beginning to fade out at the turn of the century. Bread had not always been made solely from wheat, for Marshall extolled the nutritive qualities of that made in Farndale from maslin, a mixture of wheat and rye, and Best described precisely the different meals used for bread, pies, and puddings.[4]

[1] Mr J. Welford, Hinderwell.
[2] Mr H. Tindall, Danby.
[3] Mr G. Russell, Kirkbymoorside.
[4] Henry Best, *Rural Economy in Yorkshire in 1641*, ed. C. B. Robinson, Surtees Society, XXXIII, 1857.

As the mills ceased to grind and dress grain for flour, the silk screens, which in any case were only in operation for a short period, fell into disrepair, and wholemeal continued to be used for a time. The miller at Bransdale used to collect weekly from the Bentleys of Moorhouses Farm about four stones of wheat and four or five sixteen-stone bags of oats and barley. When ground and returned, the oatmeal and barley meal were fed to stock and the wheat meal was in two types, one with the *sloughs* (husks) left in which was used for turn cakes. During the First World War the Cornforths of Mountain Ash, Glaisdale, took wheat to be ground at Stonegate Mill near Lealholm, and received back a coarse brownish flour, bran and *sharps* (pollard).

The many water mills and a few windmills, often empty and ruinous, are to be seen in almost all the villages and dales, mute reminders of their former importance as centres of trade and activity. Dependent on the water supply, many were small with two pairs of stones. Pickering had seven mills; many closed in the 1930s, but Ruswarp and Thornton-le-Dale, both large and modernized, and a very few others continue.[1]

Rievaulx Mill may be taken as an example. It has been disused since Mr Arthur Robinson retired in 1961. He followed three generations of his family who as was usual with small mills also had land and stock. The mill had three pairs of stones, two French Burr for grinding wheat for flour and one Derbyshire Peak for *proggin* (cattle food). Arthur Robinson as a boy travelled round with the miller's waggon and horses delivering meal and collecting corn. On Saturdays farmers themselves often brought corn to be ground, and for some the miller *moultered*— that is, took so much corn in lieu of the price for grinding. Sometimes after harvest as long as there was water they worked all night, and at other less busy times there were millstones to dress (*see plates* 138–42) and to bridge (set level), a delicate task. 'You could tell by the humming sound if all was well.' Other millers speak of judging the grinding by the smell.

[1] Mr T. Dodsworth, Pickering.

CHEESE-MAKING UTENSILS

1 Cheese press, formerly at Plumtree Farm, Danbydale, now at Danby Museum (8 feet 9 inches across at the widest part). 2 Typical milk can. 3 Measure for rennet. 4 Cheese kettle. 5 Chesfords and sinker (lid). 6 Curd cutter from Newtondale (Danby Museum). 7 Cheese press at Nook House, Danbydale, similar to one formerly at Cragg House Farm, Danbydale, now at R.F.M. 8 Grinder to fix on a table. 9 Curd cutter.

2, 3, 4, 5, 8 and 9 used by the Mortimers at Dale View, Westerdale.

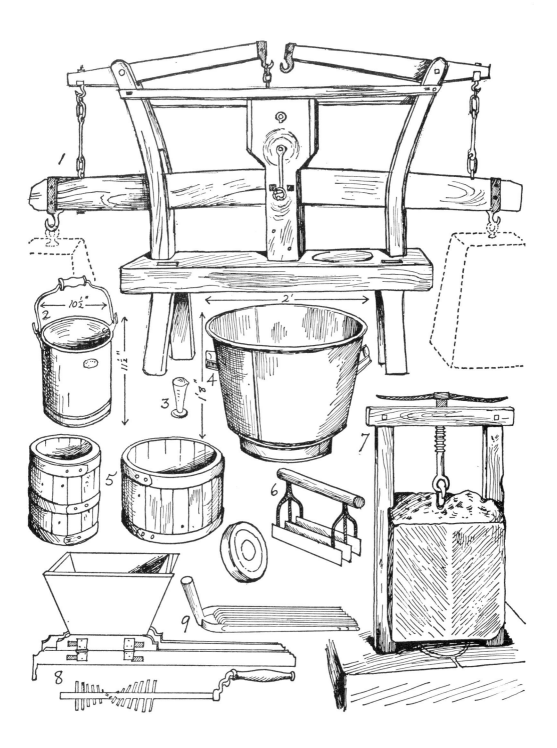

In the dales of Glaisdale, Fryup, Danby, and Westerdale the making of Cleveland cheese, similar in type to Wensleydale, formed part of the economy. The Raws of Ajalon Farm, Great Fryup, well known for their cheese, may be taken as an example. They made on average two tons a year in 4-lb. to 7-lb. cheeses. 'We put the copper on every day that ever came,' they say. 'We were up early and still going at cheese-making at night. You didn't expect anything else.' The blue sold 'like ripe cherries'.

Mr Raw described how the day before Castleton Fair, held once a year for cheese in October, they cleaned out a waggon, filled the bottom with straw, and packed the same sized cheeses together. Laden waggons used to line the main street; but 'the last time I went to Castleton I couldn't get a bargain'. As elsewhere, the making of cheese on the farms diminished after the formation of the Milk Marketing Board and ended altogether about 1946.

An example of the thriftiness of those days of sixty or seventy years ago is that of a family who brought up twelve children on a smallholding of fourteen acres near Hawsker. They kept a useful mare and a pony, a few cows, and forty, increased to eighty, sheep on the adjoining stray. Each Saturday the parents loaded up the pony and trap with farm and garden produce to sell in Whitby. Riding the pony the father travelled with an entire (stallion) on a round as far as Filey, and each year they cut and led from near Lilla Cross thirteen waggon loads of turves, enough for the fuel supply for the year. The children were apprenticed to joiners and cobblers; some went to Liverpool, others became policemen. When after forty years the father retired, he had saved £400, considered to be a lot of money. It lasted him until he died aged eighty-four and even then there was a little left.

The fortunes of another family have been told us by Mr Isaac Ventress of Wombleton and his brother, John, who died aged eighty-nine in 1970. Their grandfather, George Ventress, a stone mason by trade, and their father started farming at Old Kiln, East Moors, a smallholding of thirty acres plus a sheep stray, rented at 2s. 6d. a week. They then moved to Old Woods, a farm of 100 acres, and from there to Hasty Bank near by, a holding of 150 acres. Here old George died at the age of ninety and from here Isaac walked three miles there and three miles back to and from school winter and summer. 'The schoolmaster was nothing but a farmer who learnt us to spell and do arithmetic.'

The Ventresses had eight sons and four daughters, and in 1903 they moved to Skiplam Grange, a 500-acre farm, near Kirkbymoorside. The first year, in spite of twenty or more neighbours coming to help on several ploughing days, the seed corn was sown late and this combined with disastrous weather resulted in the loss of all their corn. Borrowing £500, they paid it back within two years. At Skiplam twenty men were employed. They had seven waggons and thirty or forty horses of different ages. Up to then they had been tenants and in 1917, by which time members of the family had scattered, they bought and moved to High Park, Kirkbymoorside.

For various reasons—the amalgamation of small farms reducing the total number, the selling of others, and the tendency of new owners to farm them themselves—removals, properly called flittings from the Old Norse *flytja*, to remove, are less common than formerly. 'Ay, we'se flitting', said the Farndale hob in the famous story of the mischievous imp whom the farmer hoped to shed by flitting. At these events neighbours offered help with horses and waggons to the outgoing tenant. 'If you liked your neighbour it was a friendly thing to do; if you didn't like him you were glad to help him go. Either way you were sure to get help.' 'You felt out of it if you didn't go to a flitting.'

Farms mostly changed hands on 25th March, 6th April or 13th May, and at the time valuations, dependent partly on the tenancy agreement, were and still are made. Mr Harrison Weighell of Appleton-le-Moors, who is a valuer as his father was before him, has described the method. Before 1900 when comparatively small sums and few items were involved, any two good men representing the waygoing and the incoming tenants (the latter paid the valuer's fee), with another man if necessary called in to act as arbitrator, valued the goods left behind.

These included the waygoing crop, *heeafed* sheep, stacks, grindstones, dipping accommodation, young fruit trees, gooseberry bushes, garden produce, fireplaces, cranes, reckons, coppers, even flags on the floor, cupboards, shelves, racks, bacon hooks, window fittings, manure and turves (the value of their cost in labour). Manure, measured by the cubic foot, was sometimes turned over by the tenant to make it look more. If the land had been limed allowance was made, and ponds, water troughs and, since about 1900, pipes and fittings for water supplies were included. When fixtures such as horse wheels and barn threshers went out of date they lost their value.

From the eighteenth century until the early years of the present century lime, used for dressing the land, was burnt on a large scale in commercial kilns situated along the limestone belt on the edge of the Vale of Pickering. As a result of the extensive use of lime affecting the soils, wheat and other grain replaced rye as the main crop of Ryedale and the moorland dales.[1] The coal for burning lime was mined on the north side of the moorlands, and in consequence a constant stream

[1] J. Tuke, *General View of Agriculture of the North Riding*, 1794, p. 35; and W. Marshall, *Rural Economy of Yorkshire*, 1788, vol. II, p. 15.

of waggons and horses plying across the moorland roads, taking coal to exchange for lime, was a feature of those times.[1]

Before the days of piped water supplies, village, farm and cottage ponds were far more numerous and essential for the watering of stock, the keeping of ducks and geese, and for purposes such as steeping straw for thatching. Some are of great age (*see plate* 37), and many no longer necessary have been filled in. The round artificial ponds, seen in different states of repair, were mostly made in the last century. Marshall records that two well-diggers and fishpond makers of Driffield discovered the art of making drinking pools about 1760, and that for many years men used to come from the Wolds to construct them. Well-kept ponds are still to be seen for instance on Appleton Common and at Silpho, near Hackness.

In the old days beyond recollection, over a hundred years ago, instead of gates made to swing on hinges, five or six wooden bars were slotted into upright stones placed at either side of a gateway. Some of these stones, now disused, may still be seen with L-shaped hollows on one and round holes on the other (*see drawing on page* 45). Even when gates were introduced a 'Sunday pole' used to be put across to prevent the horses not working on that day from damaging them.

Every farm had a saw-horse, which usually consisted of stone walls built on three sides of a pit dug in the side of a hill and topped with a timber framework, so that trees or logs, first squared with an axe, could be rolled down on to it (*see plate* 39). Before the top and bottom sawyers started work with a whip-saw, they marked the log by rubbing a length of string with a burnt stick, and, holding this tight at each end, plucked it so that it snapped down leaving a black line as a guide for sawing.

A relic, the use of which is not remembered, is the beam press, of which five base stones in or near Eskdale have survived.[2] By means of a beam wedged at one end in a tree or a wall and pressed down at the other end by a weight, leverage was applied on to a container holding crab apples. The juice ran down on to the base stone, which was scored with lines to conduct it into a receptacle. By this means verjuice, a kind of vinegar, was made.

Two drinks of the moorlands are *botchet* (mead) and gale beer (*see plates* 26, 27). Botchet is described in the chapter on bees. For gale beer, often drunk in the hay and harvest fields, a bunch of gale (bog myrtle) is scalded with a gallon of water and 1½ to 2 lb. of sugar, a lemon cut in half, and a teaspoonful of cream of tartar

[1] J. T. Sewell, *Account of Medieval Roads*, 1923; and J. Ford, *Reminiscences of Danby Parish*, 1953.
[2] Seen at Underpark Farm, near Lealholm, Postgate and Mountain Ash Farms, Glaisdale, at Danby Museum and one at Lealholmside.

added. When cold 1 oz. of yeast on a slice of toast is floated on it, and after twenty-four hours it is strained and bottled.

The diarist F. C. Dawson records in 1843 seeing spinning wheels and wool cards in use in a kitchen in Rosedale. More recently 'A girl in a hard-working family was always expected to be able to knit a pair of stockings and make a man's shirt'. At Helmsley and Kirkbymoorside and the villages round about a

The old method of barring gateways by slotting poles in round holes in a stone post at one side, and dropping them into L-shaped recesses (as pictured) in a post on the other.

flax spinning and weaving industry formerly flourished. Soft bonnets were worn by the women of a former generation for warmth in winter and for protection against the sun in summer, and may still be seen at Staithes (*see plate* 29). In line with the general frugality some men plaited straw mattresses for children's beds, and *bull fronts* (large tussocks of grass) were utilized in church as hassocks.[1]

An example of a woman of the old school, Grannie Beeforth (born in the 1860s) and her long and spirited life are remembered by her daughter Mrs H. Tindall of Danby. When she married, her husband (who worked for her father) brought home 10*s.* a week. They had five children and eventually took Fir Tree Farm,

[1] *Gwerin*, vol. I.

Fryup, where Grannie was to live for forty years. Until the children were about eight, she made all the boys' suits from old material, and she baked bread in a brick oven heated with peat or turf.

On Saturdays she took butter, eggs, chickens, honey and beeswax to Whitby market. She broke in horses, and in 1918, when a neighbouring family had 'flu, she fed their stock and milked fourteen cows. She rode from place to place on a pony and acted as midwife at births and laid people out when they died—all without payment. She made mead, wines and home-made remedies such as Mother Seigel's syrup for indigestion and tonics taken in the spring and autumn; and she inhaled an infusion of wild sage for quinsy, which she suffered from for years. She died aged ninety-five in the early 1950s as the old life also was coming to an end.

PLOUGHING AND SOWING

TOWARDS the end of the eighteenth century the open common fields surrounding every village, mentioned in Domesday Book, on the edge of the Vale of Pickering had been enclosed. None of the dales except Eskdale and Westerdale is included in that survey and only the latter had vestiges of a field system.

Marshall says that no straightforward rotation of crops was practised in the Vale. 'Every man follows the dictates of his own judgement, and subjects his arable land to such uses best suited to the general economy of his farm in the given year'.[1] Except when restricted as on the Feversham estate to seeds, oats, turnips, corn, this flexibility continued.

In Eskdale the usual four-course system was generally stipulated in farm agreements, and is well remembered. The sequence followed was seeds (grass) the first year, oats the second, root crop the third, and mixed barley and oats the fourth. By undersowing the barley and oats with grass or clover seed to grow after the corn had been harvested the cycle began again. 'We wanted to leave the land better than we found it' was the consideration. This continued up to the years between the wars when, because of government intervention and the need to grow more food, a further corn crop was introduced giving a five-year rotation.[2]

Mr B. Frank described the latter as practised at Hutton-le-Hole: 'In the first year the swarth [grass] was made into hay and eaten; next year we sowed and harvested oats; in the back end as the land was getting poorer we *scaled* muck on to the oat stubble and ploughed it in. In November we sowed wheat. In the third year the wheat was harvested. In that winter the land, now very dirty, was laid *fauf* [fallow] and in the following spring ploughed and ploughed; in June we drilled for turnips, most of which were eaten by sheep which manured the land. Lastly in the fifth year we ploughed as light as possible because the manure was on top, sowed barley, undersown with seeds', thus as before starting the rotation again.

For ploughing, a horseman had his own pair of horses which were broken in

[1] *Rural Economy of Yorkshire*, 1788, vol. 1, p. 296.
[2] Mr H. Tindall and Mr F. Raw, formerly of Fryup.

together. As one walked on the furrow and the other on the land side, they were used to their own positions. Some men taught them when they were young to go on either side. 'It was t'awkwardest thing you could find if you put both on to sides they didn't like.'

Some older farmers remember the practice of ploughing 'yardlands'—a practice deriving from the *rigg and furr* (ridge and furrow) of the strips of the open fields.[1] Yardlands were five to eight yards wide, latterly eight, raised in the centre (the rigg) and separated by hollows (the furrs). They were formed by setting the rigg in the same place over the old one year after year. As the mouldboard of the plough always throws the furrow to the right, by starting ploughing in the centre of the rigg up and down, up and down, clockwise, the furrows were all turned inwards towards the middle, thus forming the raised riggs. Where these met every eight yards the furrows were turned away from each other, thus making hollows—the furrs.

Several advantages were thought to result. The furrs, filling with water, drained the land, and when dry they gave shelter to sheep. In the day of the scythe grass was mown up on to the dry rigg; and the actual grazing surface was reckoned to be increased by one acre in every four. On a Sunday morning the men went round viewing everybody's yardlands to see if they were straight. Although rapidly disappearing, the characteristic hump-backed lines of rigg and furr may still be seen in pastures near the villages along the edge of the Vale of Pickering.

With the advent of machinery a level field became the objective. It still had to be ploughed in sections, but riggs were now eighteen to twenty yards wide, separated by throwing-out pieces (called flinging-out in Eskdale) of the same width. Depending on its size a field might have three riggs and two throwing-out pieces. Each time the field was newly ploughed the riggs were moved to the furrows in the centre of the throwing-out pieces, thus as will be seen keeping the surface level.

When the ploughman started, he measured off the headlands (where the plough turned) four or five yards from the baulk (a bank on which the hedge usually grew) all round the field and put in sticks taken from the hedge. Then taking three or four more, often peeled, he set them up in a line as markers across the field (setting the rigg) and began ploughing so that the horses passed one on either side of the sticks: 'They knew.' He continued 'gathering', that is, ploughing up and down clockwise turning the furrow towards the centre (*see plates* 72–5). For the throwing-out piece he ploughed round and round from the outside anti-clockwise. However many there were in a field, riggs were always ploughed first.

[1] Mr H. Tindall, Mr F. Raw, Fryup; Mr I. Ventress, Wombleton; Mr J. Skaife, Pickering; Mr A. Watson, Kirkbymoorside.

72. *Mr L. Barnes, Yatts Brow Farm, near Newton-on-Rawcliffe. Ploughing a rigg (1930s).*

73. *Ploughing a throwing-out piece at Fadmoor (1926).*

74. *Ploughing with a pair of Cleveland Bays and a North Cave plough. Probably at Lealholm Hall* (c. *1900?*).

75. *Mr John Maw, Low Mill, Farndale, ploughing with Queenie and a John Wood plough* (c. *1905*).

76. *Teams of horses in Helmsley market place on the way to a ploughing day* (*1912*).

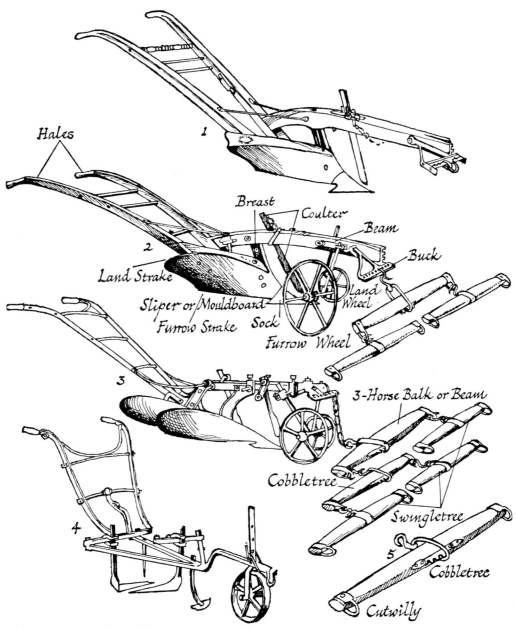

Hales

Breast
Coulter
Beam
Buck
Land Strake
Sliper or Mouldboard
Furrow Strake
Sock
Land Wheel
Furrow Wheel

3-Horse Balk or Beam
Cobbletree
Swingletree
Cobbletree
Cutwilly

IMPLEMENTS FOR CULTIVATION

1 North Cave swing plough with 'H. Benson Maker Ruswarp' on the mouldboard. (Postgate Farm, Glaisdale.) 2 North Cave wheeled plough. The plough has 'W. E. Saunders Maker North Cave' on the land side of the breast (R.F.M.). 3 Double furrow plough and horse balks (R.F.M.). 4 Scruffler (Old Byland Grange). 5 Cobbletree.

For grassland and seedland he ploughed a close rigg—that is, on the first turn-about taking a small furrow and on the second *lapping* ordinary furrows over the little ones so that they just met in the middle of the rigg. There had to be no *troves* (turves) showing. For stubble and fallow he made an open rigg (splitting the rigg) by ploughing a turnabout once anti-clockwise so that the furrows fell away to right and left, and on the second round going clockwise throwing them inwards to overlap the first furrows and meet. Similarly the last three furrows, sometimes the last one, were scored out by tilting the plough to make little furrows.

Because of the miles of walking entailed behind the usual single furrow plough and a pair of horses up and down turnabout by turnabout day in day out, plough-ing was often a lad's work. Although this did not apply to the dales, in the Wolds men could be tired out by middle age and their feet had suffered. If he had other jobs to do, a man with two horses ploughed less than an acre a day, and on large farms in particular each kept to his own plough.

Ploughing was indeed an art dependent on knowledge and skill. The plough-man could adjust the *buck* (shackle) for the different pull of the two horses which he drove with plough cords, often called whip strings, held on top of the *hales* (handles), and he could also set the wheels for ploughing fallow or barley or oats, which all needed different depths of furrow. He always carried a few wooden wedges for a wood plough (or iron wedges for an iron plough) in his pocket to fix the coulter in position.

In awkward shaped fields *gays* or *gairs* (triangular pieces) had to be run off. Lastly the headlands were ploughed, and for the last furrow the horses might be harnessed single file, and the next year they came round in the opposite direction. It used to be said that if there had been a new addition to the family, you took another furrow from the baulk; and in those thrifty days old men were known to dig out the corners with spades.[1]

As we shall show later, wagers were a feature of early nineteenth-century life, and one man, a village or a district used publicly to challenge another in plough-ing matches. From these there developed in the 1840s and 1850s organized open ploughing competitions.[2] One held at Sinnington in 1859 attracted sixty-seven entries in classes for farmers' sons, for boys under and men over eighteen using swing and wheeled ploughs,[3] and another held at Spout House on 21st February, 1907, was the jubilee competition of the Bilsdale Ploughing and Hedge-Cutting

[1] Mr B. Frank.
[2] *Malton Messenger*, 21st March 1857, and *Whitby Gazette*, 16th January 1858.
[3] *Malton Messenger*, 22nd January 1859.

Society, at which all the prize winners used John Wood ploughs.[1] A champion ploughman might be away for a week competing in different matches. To round off these and similar events a dinner followed.

Mr Isaac Ventress remembers seeing 'forty to a hundred competitors in a field. You started at 8 a.m. and finished at 4 p.m. The plough was set to plough square—that is, eight inches deep and an eight-inch furrow. You took several socks and coulters, using the ones most suitable, and you drew lots for places all staked out and numbered.

'For exhibition work like this the ploughman fixed a V-shaped scratcher on the land wheel, and he started by making two marks absolutely straight up and down 16 inches apart. Also each man had a small chain attached to the beam; this tucked in the grass as he went along. Behind it on another chain trailed a glass boat that sealed up the joint (by pulling the grass underneath). These boats, about 2 feet long and flat on top, were specially made at glass works. [Or the ploughman might use a wedge-shaped steel boat fastened to the slipe with a chain.] The judge looked for solidity as well as straightness. "You could run water in a straight line down a furrow."'

The other communal ploughing event—ploughing days—when to show good-will neighbours joined together to help a newcomer, harks back to the boon days of the medieval manor. At these the lord provided the food, as did the farmer at a ploughing day. In times past, races used to follow after the work was finished and someone always sang the song ending with the chorus, 'I'll swear and I'll vow, that we're all jolly fellows what follows the plough.'

'The new man went round', says Mr F. Raw, 'and asked if you would give him a day. This was then fixed. He set his headlands and riggs so that when they all came they knew where to start. Brasses and hames were polished up, and it was who had the smartest turnout. Those near at hand brought their ploughs on sledges and the others on carts. They fettled a big table up in the kitchen for dinner, and I remember, but only once, that each man had a half crown under his plate.'

A ploughing day at Gill Beck, Glaisdale, held on 19th March 1905, is perpetuated in rhyme using the various terms employed in ploughing and the well-known names of local men—Leng, Winspear, Bonas, Hebron, Harrison, Duck, Dale and Faubert. With their horses—Snep, Johnnie, Punch, Smiler, Darling and others—they went to *felly*, that is to plough the fallow. If this were stubble it was *quarted* by ploughing across the direction of the previous ploughing. One

1 *Yorkshire Herald*, 23rd February 1907.

man had his horses 'coupled wide', and another was likely to 'get in the lock' on a narrow ridge (to turn too sharply).[1] Ploughing days finished in the 1930s.

Seed corn was often saved, and new seed bought for one field. Similarly hay seeds were shaken out of a pile of hay on the barn floor, then passed through riddles. Within memory seed corn was dressed with urine and lime and it is still treated with chemicals in barrel churns no longer used for butter-making. Every farm had wooden measures to gauge quantities of grain. When one was filled the corn was struck off, and tipped into a sack until enough had accumulated for the field to be sown. The amounts varied from two to two and a half bushels to an acre for wheat and three to four for barley and oats (*see plate* 77).

The traditional time for sowing was in general from 21st March to 21st April, and assuming that conditions were favourable the first week in April was always sowing time in Farndale. But old people used to say 'the first seed-time after February was the right one'.

Drills were uncommon at the turn of the century.[2] Many remember sowing by hand, and a few still do so (*see plates* 81 *and* 82). Choosing a quiet day, the sower sows the headlands first and then walks down the seams of the ploughing. He rhythmically matches the stride to the swing of the arm, and giving a flick sends the corn forth in a fan shape. Using two hands he covers a breadth of two yards and takes half an hour to sow an acre. Some preferred to use one hand, going down the field and back in the same place, so that they did not miss or *breed* (overlap) the corn. Harrowing followed at once 'to make a good mould and *hap* the seed'.

In the old days it was often women's and children's work to drop turnip seed into the seams of the ploughing, and the following method was employed at Glaisdale Head sixty years ago. The two bottom corners of an apron were knotted together, and a cow tie, made of plaited hair from a cow's tail, was hitched from the knot and tied round the waist. Turnip seed mixed with ashes and peat was placed in the pouch thus formed, and the mixture dropped into every third seam.[3] For small seeds hand drills were used, or they were sown by finger and thumb or very commonly with the fiddle drill (*see plates* 78–80, 83). The latter is still seen.

An implement that disappeared before the First World War used at this time of year was the land scrubber, a clod crusher consisting of several two-inch planks bolted together arranged like weather boarding. Besides these, oak rollers are remembered in Farndale, followed by stone rollers (*see plate* 86), often preferred to the plain iron or the later Cambridge rollers with discs.

[1] Lent to us by Mr W. L. Thompson, Glaisdale.
[2] Rev J. C. Atkinson, *Forty Years in a Moorland Parish* (1891), 1923 edition, p. 8 fn.
[3] Mr E. Atkinson, Raw Farm.

After sowing, the stones were picked off the fields, usually women's and children's work. 'We wore big coarse aprons and piled them in heaps; then they were carted on the farm roads.' 'When I was a child it was our job to pick stones after sowing about Easter week. If we finished by Good Friday we could go to Glaisdale Head tea party.' 'We stoned the grass fields an' all especially if they had been manured. They allus used ter *look* corn [seek weeds] too. Yer *looker* was like a hoe but smaller. It's all slipped today.'[1]

[1] Mrs E. Burns, Fryup; Mrs H. Tindall, formerly of Fryup; Mr R. Welford, Glaisdale.

77. *Mr J. L. Thompson and Mr W. L. Thompson, Postgate Farm, Glaisdale, demonstrate measuring seed corn by striking off the corn in a half bushel measure.*

78–80. *Mr W. Leckenby sowing small seed—Italian rye grass and kale—with the finger and thumb in Barn Field on Sieve Green Farm, Bilsdale. At each end he made a mark as a guide to where he had been so that he could see the 'feetings'. He sows the seed with a flick on the forward movement, and covers two yards at a time. It took him an hour and a half to sow two acres.*

81. *Mr S. Halder, wearing braces holding the hopper, sows oats on Raw Farm, near Robin Hood's Bay.*

82. *Mr E. Atkinson demonstrates sowing with a seed box which he used until recently on Raw Farm.*

83. *Mr H. Tindall, Head House, Fryup, using a fiddle-drill to re-seed with rye grass, Timothy, cocksfoot, white clover and rape. He sows every three yards 30 lb. to the acre. The bag holds 10 lb.*

84. *Mr F. Nellis and Mr N. Nellis harrowing for wheat with Darkie and Prince. Darkie, four years old, had only been yoked once before (1964).*

85. *Mr E. Bowes harrowing with an iron harrow on Corner Farm, Wrelton (Mr Braithwaite's) (c. 1938).*

86. *Mr C. Dawson and Toby, Delves Farm, Egton Bridge, rolling with a stone roller.*

87. *Mr C. R. Dykes, North Wood Farm, Chop Gate, Bilsdale, leading muck. The raised paved way behind is the scaife (1945).*

POTATOES

88. *Mr W. L. Thompson and his family setting potatoes and sowing fertilizer on Postgate Farm, Glaisdale (c. 1953).*

89. *Mr H. Worley, Lamplands Farm, Egton, with Violet and a young horse rowing up potatoes.*

HARVESTING

WITHIN memory corn was harvested by a team of workers in a manner little changed since the Middle Ages. It was a season when farmers recruited extra staff, when sickles and *lyes* (scythes) were sharpened, and when sandhorns, *strickles* (sharpeners), leggings, rakes and forks were fettled in readiness. A great force of people—women, children, men of all sorts of occupations—set forth into the fields.

In 1641 Best described how on his farm on the Wolds both men and women sheared wheat with the sickle whilst men mowed oats and barley with the scythe. But Marshall in his day records that in our area wheat was being sheared by women only.[1] Half a century later in Fylingdales 'the system of mowing, instead of shearing, corn has diminished the demand for [women's] labour in harvest'.[2] Yet in the middle of the next century wheat was still described in the *Malton Messenger* as 'ready for the sickle'.[3] Although not clear it would appear that the scythe was gradually being adopted for mowing all corn. By 1890 the mechanical reaper was in general use, and by 1920 most farmers had obtained new or second-hand self-binders.

Here and there the sickle continued to be used.

'When I was a lad in the 1890s women used to shear. Two good strokes right round and they had a *shaff* [sheaf] which they held under their left arms. They always wore leather leggings on their left legs for protection.'[4] 'A sickle had a little iron bow made of pliable wire attached to stop the corn from falling down. With it you could *wap* [strike off] a shaff at twice.'[5]

'I remember an old man, Constantine Abraham, "Owd Con" of Ellers House, Fryup, a smallholding of fifteen acres. He kept five or six cows and two

[1] *Rural Economy of Yorkshire*, 1788, vol. 1, p. 387. Also J. Tuke, *General View of Agriculture of the North Riding*, 1794, p. 37.
[2] *Reports on the Employment of Women and Children in Agriculture*, 1843, reprint 1968, p. 365.
[3] *Malton Messenger*, 14th August 1858.
[4] Mr I. Ventress, Wombleton.
[5] Mr J. Welford, Hinderwell.

pigs. He always sheared wheat. He drew the corn backwards with a cane [of willow or hazel] in his left hand bringing it round to his left hip. Then he struck with the sickle. The cane held the corn in place and with two or three movements he had a shaff. He kept it all against himself and tied as he went along.'[1]

Mowing corn with the scythe is most generally remembered. The lye in full *graith* (fitted up) for mowing corn or grass had a pole of willow 7 to 9 feet long bought from ironmongers or blacksmiths, a blade about 4 feet 6 inches long, perhaps made by W. Tyzack at the Abbeydale Works, Sheffield, a curved and a straight nib made of ash, a grass nail, wedges, and a strickle of green oak, or sometimes lime. For corn a bow or cradle was attached. This was a length of hazel, or briar with the thorns rubbed off, fastened down by staples and supported by a standard (thin iron rod); *see page 56 and plate 99*.[2] On a scythe correctly fitted up, the distance from the tip of the blade to the heel, from the heel to the lower nib and from the nib back to the tip of the blade had to be equal.

'When using a bow you tilted it each time you finished your batt. My father cut a six-foot *breead* [breadth] and a foot forward each strike. If it was a good crop, you could get a shaff straight on to t'band.'[3] Others say only a five-foot breead. 'My family has mown Lockton churchyard for over a hundred years. My father once mew nine acres of corn in three days. He could mow as fast as he could walk. A mower's born not made.'[4]

Before haytime began silver sand or soft stone to be brayed fine was collected for coating the strickle. 'My father always used to go to Ladgill near Hawnby for stone.'[5] 'We went from Goathland House to near Ellerbeck Bridge on the Whitby-Pickering road. We opened out the stone and covered it up again, so that others shouldn't find it.'[6] Some used resin or common soap to smear on the strickle, but the old way was to rub on swine grease—a thick piece of fat from the loin of a pig. 'At a pig killing my old uncle always took a piece of fat and rolled it up with string just the right size to fit the horn and stored it in a cupboard. When the time came he cut a piece off as required.'[7]

[1] Mr F. Raw, Ainthorpe.
[2] Mr W. W. Featherstone, Lastingham; and also notes of Mr J. Weatherill, lent by Mr G. Weatherill, Sleights.
[3] Mr S. Shaw, Riddings, Westerdale.
[4] Mr B. Wilson, Lockton.
[5] Mr Jim Ainsley, Helmsley.
[6] Mr John Agar, Pickering.
[7] Mr J. Atkinson, Hartoft.

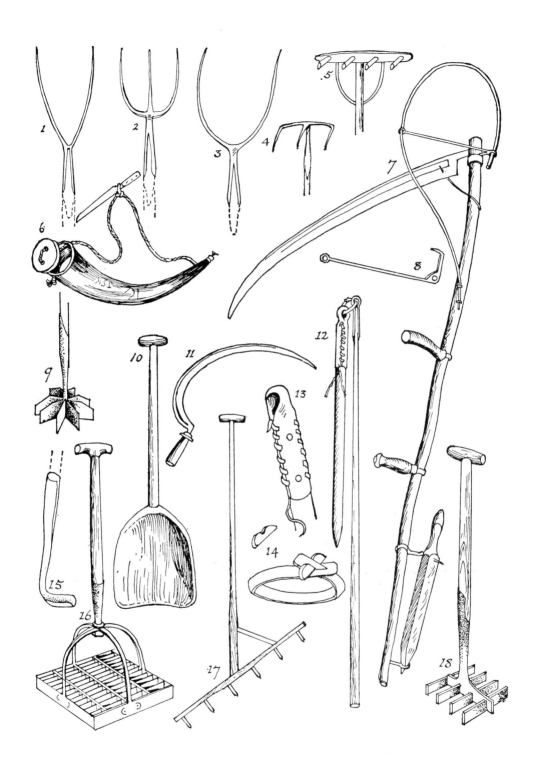

At the wide end of the sandhorn a space held the fat and at the thin end a plug kept in the sand (*see drawing on page 56*). A length of string threaded through cap and plug enabled the mower to carry it over his shoulder, and the knife tied to the string was used to scrape off old grease and press on new grease and sand. Two opposite sides were sanded at a time so that there were two newly-sanded coarse sides to start on and two finer used ones to finish with.

To test for sharpness a sixpence might be pressed flat on the edge of the blade, which should be able to be lifted three times over the shoulder.[1] Or put a little differently: 'A good mower could walk across a field and carry a sixpence on the blade.'

Mowing, like ploughing, lent itself to wagers. Sometimes twelve matched themselves against another twelve to mow twelve acres of grass in the quickest time. Or, an original contest was that between Mrs Margaret Wallace and Mr Thomas Magson both of Wrelton to mow half an acre of corn for £1 a side; the winner to distribute the stake amongst the cottagers in flour.[2]

Usually mowers each cut about an acre to an acre and a half of corn in a day. (Best says three acres of oats.) In the last century it was reckoned that four threaves and four sheaves, that is 100 sheaves, was a decent day's work for a good mower with a boy to help tie up.[3] The mowers were accompanied by children to tie bands, by liers-out (usually women), by binders of sheaves *scramping* (tying up) and a stooker. 'I've heard 'em say that Estill Peacock had three scythes, three liers-out, three tying up and one to stook. Ten on 'em in all.'[4]

The boys tied bands by taking two bunches of corn, dexterously twisting their heads into a knot. If the straw was a good length they didn't always bother to make cross bands, but twisted the heads and by wrapping another piece of straw over, a knot resulted. The band had to be laid in the exact place so that the lier-

---

[1] Mr W. W. Featherstone, Lastingham.
[2] *Malton Messenger*, 11th August 1855; 23rd August 1856.
[3] Notes of Mr J. Weatherill.
[4] Mr G. Agar, North Ghyll, Farndale.

FARM TOOLS

1 Blacksmith-made fork. 2 Muck fork. 3 Straw fork. 4 and 5 Gathering rakes. 6 Grease and sandhorn for strickle. 7 Lye (scythe) in full graith i.e. fully set up with bow for mowing corn. 8 Standard (iron rod) which supports the bow. 9 Star for cutting turnips. 10 Wooden grain shovel. 11 Sickle. 12 Flail. 13 Flail cap. 14 Leather loop and wooden wedge which join the flail handstaff and swipple. 15 Turnip scoop. 16 Fautering iron or barley humbler. 17 Laying-off rake for ratrap reaper. 18 Turnip cutter (R.F.M.).

out, using a gathering rake, put together a sheaf with a minimum of movement. The band-maker aimed to be three ahead (*see plate* 101 *and drawings on page* 56).

The tier-up following on suffered from sore knuckles, often exacerbated by thistles. In the old method of tying with a 'wreath' knot made by twisting the straw round three times, using both hands and tucking the end under the band, he had to bend to work on the ground. But at some time this was replaced by 'waud wapping' introduced from the Wolds, whereby the two ends of the straw band were twisted together with one hand and tucked under so that the tier-up held the sheaf against his knee. 'You could wap as quick as you walked.'

If it was not laid, corn was easier to mow than grass, and the method employed differed. 'You mowed grass outwards and corn inwards,' and put your left foot forward for grass and your right for corn.[1] 'You scythe corn according to the wind. You mustn't push it back against the wind. My Dad used to say, "You must walk up to the corn. Stand right up to it".'[2] 'Never bend your back to mow. Set your lye so that you can mow straight up. You had to go by the sway. If the sway changed you had to change with it. It must be falling from you against the corn. You weren't worth your salt if you couldn't mow.'[3]

Men with other work often mowed at night. 'My grandfather went round mowing and once got a grandfather clock as part payment.'[4] 'My father and Jim James went to Green Farm and were told to mow Five Roods which was three acres. They mew it in a day and got five shillings apiece. They used to mow for haytime here, then went on to the Wolds, usually on the same farm year after year, to mow corn where it ripened sooner than in the dales, then they came back to Egton and mew here.'[5] 'Father had a little field. He would go on a Saturday morning, him with the scythe and the two lads. It had to be mown, tied up, stooked and *knagged* [raked] before he went to bed.'[6]

The first grass mower to come into the Whitby district was tried out at Hagget House in 1861,[7] but in general these machines appeared in the 1890s. At Goathland House the wife of an old helper found great fault with them as she thought there would be no work for Jack. About the same time the first combined grass and corn mowing machines usually made by Kearsley, Samuelson or Bamlett, arrived

[1] Mr John Ainsley, Bilsdale. See also W. Marshall, *Rural Economy of Yorkshire*, 1788, vol. II, p. 399.
[2] Mr S. Shaw, Westerdale.
[3] Mr C. R. Dykes, Marton.
[4] Mr T. W. Ventress, Egton.
[5] Mr A. Agar, Egton.
[6] Mr J. Skaife, Pickering.
[7] T. H. English, *Whitby Prints*, vol. II, 1931.

in the dales. These were adjusted to a fast gear for cutting grass and a lower gear for cutting corn. Every new machine was regarded with suspicion. 'She'll never go,' they said, 'it's ower wet for her.'

Then followed the 'put-off' or 'ratrap' reaper made by several firms including Bamlett, Mattison, Kearsley and the Albion Foundry at Leigh in Lancashire. The first in Farndale came to North Ghyll Farm before 1900. At the time regarded as a great advance, the put-off stayed in use here and there until the 1950s. Often three farms joined up and shared the reaper among them, or a farmer hired his out for £1 a day.

The put-off cut a breead of 4 feet to 4 feet 6 inches. A man walking beside it drove the horses, whilst a second man sitting on the seat pressed a lever with his foot to bring up a gate of wooden lats. When sufficient corn for a sheaf had collected he let it down, and wielding a laying-off rake he slid the corn off in a tidy heap (see plate 100 and drawing on page 56).

Binding was not part of the process so that a gang still had to follow behind tying up the sheaves to clear the way for the next round. There might be a dozen people in the field engaged in tying and stooking, or four or five each taking a side of the mown corn. 'I loved the harvest. I used to tie round the field. All had their length to tie and if one was slow he had to be shifted on.'[1]

About 1900 self-binders arrived. Bought either new or second-hand, they were mostly Massey-Harris (Canadian) or Deering and McCormick (American), and after fifty years and more some of them are still running.

'Nothing looked nicer than a grand field of corn stooked'; and it is still possible to see this sight. Stooking started from the outside of a field and ended in the middle. Men and women usually working in pairs took up two sheaves at a time, and, thrusting the butts into the stubble, propped them against each other. Eight sheaves or often ten or twelve made a stook. A hole through the bottom allowed for the passage of air. It should 'smoke through'.

The tying up of the last sheaf marked the end of harvesting and the vestiges of a once impressive ceremony are remembered. 'For the last sheaf everybody was there and each tied a band round it. At night my father cut them all loose so that the corn could dry. For the last tea-time mell cakes were brought into the field, cut in four, split, buttered, and sprinkled with sugar and nutmeg. There was a milk bucket full of tea, and fun with the rabbits at the end.'[2]

The meal was the *kern* supper which followed the end of harvesting, as the mell supper followed the end of leading. The first was so called because for centuries

[1] Mr T. Frankland, Farndale.
[2] Mr F. Raw, Ainthorpe.

cream in a churn had been brought on to the field. Best describes this treat after harvesting when, following meat and apple pies, cream is brought in platters 'and every one a spoon, then after all hot cakes and ale. . . . Some will cut their cake and put it into the cream, and this feast is called the cream-potte or cream-kitte.'[1] Canon Atkinson records the phasing out of this ancient custom when he says that in his day a bowl of new milk or even frumity did duty for the cream.[2]

---

[1] One of these writers remembers being given a plateful of sour cream to be eaten with a spoon at a *seter* in Jordal, near Stalheim, Norway, in 1939.
[2] Rev. J. C. Atkinson, *A Glossary of the Cleveland Dialect*, 1868; and *Forty Years in a Moorland Parish*, 1891, 1923 edition page 240.

HAY HARVEST

90. *Scythemen: Mr Watson Peirson and Mr Harry Spenceley at Yatt's Farm, Rosedale (c. 1900).*

91. *Mr H. Cook, Dale Head, Westerdale, mowing grass with Bonny and Sam and a double-horse mower in Anthony Field next to the moor (1938).*

92. *Haymaking on the Duncombe Park estate, Helmsley. A pair of oxen draws the load of hay, and a horse draws the large sweep, although oxen were used with this. Note the large labour force* (c. *1890*).

93. *The Agars of Stakesby Vale Farm, Four Lane Ends, near Whitby, stacking hay* (c. *1900*).

94. *Mr E. Atkinson and Mr R. Atkinson, Raw Farm, layzband with a single row hand-drill to sow turnip seed.*

TURNIPS

95. *Mr P. Taylor, Riddings, Westerdale, demonstrates using a stamp turnip cutter made by Ord and Maddison. Used for generations, it was replaced by the rotary disc slicer early in this century.*

96. *Mr H. Wheldon and Mr W. Ferguson, also Laddie, singling swedes on Carlton Park Farm, near East Moors. Formerly there might be seven or eight men in a string.*

SWEDES

97. *Mr and Mrs A. Hugill, Ewe Cote, Farndale, taking up swedes. He is using a drag to pick them up and she is slashing with a knife.*

98. *Mowing corn and tying sheaves in a field called Band Contest, on Yatt's Farm, Rosedale. Two men are using gathering rakes and two are mowing. Mr James Peirson (Jim at Yatt) wears a hat and the mower on the right is Mr Harry Spenceley (before 1900).*

99. *Either George Readman or Thomas Harrison (known as Tommy Mowman), Lealholmside, carrying a lye (scythe) with a bow and a strickle, and a gathering rake in his right hand (c. 1900).*

HARVEST   100. *The Readmans of Lealholm Hall and helpers stop for 'lowance time. George Readman sits on a put-off or ratrap reaper. The lats, raised and lowered by a lever worked by the foot, collected (but did not tie) sufficient corn for a sheaf. The rake resting on Readman's knee was of a specific design to rake the corn off the lats (c. 1900).*

101. *Mr and Mrs L. Frank and Mrs A. Hugill demonstrate tying sheaves and using a gathering rake.*

102. *Mr J. Wass, Horn End Farm, reaping oats in West Gill, Farndale* (c. *1939*).

REAPING

103. *The Hugills and the Franks reaping with a tractor and a Massey-Harris self-binder and stooking on Ewe Cote Farm, Farndale.*

104. *Leading corn on a waggon in Wood Top Field, Lealholm Hall* (c. *1900*).

LEADING

105. *Mr C. Lyth, Benwell House, Lealholm, building an eke (stack). This type of corn stack was built six to seven yards long by three to four yards wide—a suitable size for half a day's threshing by machine.*

STACKING

THE stooks of corn stood out in the fields 'while the church bells rang twice'—that is, for about a fortnight. If available three waggons, each drawn by one horse on flat land, were used for leading—one being loaded in the field, one at the stack, and the third travelling from field to stack. A forker, who tossed up two sheaves at a time, kept a loader going, and in the stack yard the loader teemed sheaves to the picker who in turn passed them to the stacker. A waggon load in the dales averaged about fifty stooks, counting ten sheaves to a stook, that is 500 sheaves.

Forks were greatly treasured. Handles were sandpapered and oiled, and when steel forks as opposed to blacksmith-made ones came in, men were known to keep them under their beds at night.

Because it was the driest part of the field leading began in the middle. First the bottom of the waggon was filled lengthways with sheaves. Then two, three or four square courses, depending on the size of the load, were laid sideways with the butts of the sheaves arranged inwards and the heads outwards on to the flanges, going round first one way then another. Lastly came the 'shipping', with heads laid to bands lengthways beginning at the front and then at the back, with a double course at each end so that a full load resembled the shape of a ship. 'When you'd topped 'em out and roped 'em down, they did look nice.'[1]

At the farm the first load was sometimes put straight away into a barn so that straw was available for making *dozzles* (stack ornaments). Pikes, small round stacks about 6 feet high to the eaves, tapering up another 3 feet to 3 feet 6 inches, were commonly built in the dales (*see plates* 106, 107). As a base, timber and brushwood were laid across *hemmells* (square stone supports), often five arranged in a circle with one in the centre (*see plate* 21). Thus mice and rats were kept out and shelter was made for hens. 'Ah've heard 'em tell that a good builder of pikes could put 100 stooks of oats on a waggon wheel. They hadn't to spring out too much or they might *shut* [shoot] out.'[2] As many as twenty well-made pikes might

[1] Mr H. Tindall, Danby and Mr J. and Mr T. Mortimer, Westerdale.
[2] Mr J. Agar, Pickering.

61

be built in the stackyard of a dales farm, and either weekly or fortnightly, one was brought into the barn to be flailed or threshed with the barn thresher.

When travelling threshing sets took over, stacks, called *ekes*, containing fourteen or eighteen waggon loads or more, large enough for half a day or a day's threshing, were made (*see plate* 105), and on large farms stacks were built in 'coupons', that is a close row, for convenience in building them and moving on the threshing machine. Apart from the pikes and the ekes, stacks might be of several shapes—bottle with straight sides, globe, and mill-topped ones, that is onion shaped, made in Farndale and especially in Cleveland.

All stacks were thatched with either straw or *seaves* (rushes), held down by straw bands, and Mr Isaac Ventress has described the method of making the bands and of thatching as he remembers it at Skiplam Grange, a large farm, earlier this century. For a round stack seven bands were usually required, naturally diminishing in length as they went up until the top one was tiny. The bottom one was a double straw band and the rest single.

First, the stack, from twenty up to sixty feet in circumference, was measured round to ascertain the length required. Oat straw, threshed with the flail and drawn on wet days, was used as the most suitable. To make it 'as soft as a glove', it was bashed against the floor, had all the feather *sliped* off, was steeped in a beck or farm pond and hung up to dry. Tight bundles were made from which a double end was brought out to put on the hook of the winder. An old man, sitting on a stool and feeding straw from a pile beside him and another man or woman or a boy spinning the winder held under his arm or her arm, spent days and days making bands.

To make the double band from two single ones, four people were necessary. One man held the winder, with both bands attached to it, supported against the bars of a gate. At the other side of the gate a second man faced the first, and behind him the full length of the single ropes away two more men, also facing the first, each had winders hooked on to the other ends of the ropes. When the first man started to spin, the second, controlling the twist with the hands, walked backwards, whilst the two farthest off walked forwards spinning the opposite way.

Lastly the rope, fastened to a gate at one end and to a horse at the other, was pulled tight. Stretched out in this way, it didn't curl up. Then it was 'lapped in big *collops* and hung up until needed'. Newly-made ropes were used on corn stacks, and when taken off, they were wrapped up and used again on hay stacks. Their perfection may be seen on plate 110.

As opposed to thatching houses, where a great thickness of straw was laid on,

106. *Nine pikes (one hidden) in the stack-yard of Wood Hill Farm, near Lealholm.*

PIKES

107. *Mr W. Dobson, Mill Lane Farm, Lealholm, thatching a pike with sieves (rushes), prods and binder twine.*

108. *Steeping straw for thatch Lealholm Hall (c. 1890s).*

109. *Mr John Ventress, Skiplam Grange, near Kirkbymoorside, thatching stacks. He is holding a wisp of straw and has rolls of straw band ready to go round against the ladder (c. 1911).*

THATCHING STACKS

110. *Mr Isaac Ventress, Skiplam Grange, and thatched stacks with dozzles and beautifully made straw bands (c. 1911).*

a thin layer was sufficient. Before thatching proper began short straws were stuck in all round the easing (the bottom of the thatch). Wisps were then placed in a breed (a course from top to bottom) tethered by the bands drawn tight, and held down by hazel prods. As the work progressed another man viewed the whole from a distance to see that all was plumb.

At the top the Ventresses pushed in a turned wooden dozzle on a long prod. The bottom edge of the thatch was cut with a very sharp easing knife about $1\frac{1}{2}$ inches from the lowest band. (The double layer at the easing held the thatch off the bole of the stack to allow room for cutting.) Lastly the bole was trimmed with a shaving knife (*see drawings on page* 6). It took two days for a man to thatch a stack, one and half for the thatching and half a day for shaving. As Isaac Ventress said, 'Nothing could fetch thatch off them stacks till the wind blew them over.' Those shown on plate 110 were special ones for show on the outside of a stackyard. Six Ventress brothers are remembered thatching one stack apiece in the front row. They won prizes of a silver cup and a gold watch for the best stackyard in the district.

Wooden or sheet metal dozzles representing a cock or a fox, or even glass bottles were used. But in general dozzles were made of straw, sometimes in the shape of birds, animals, a cross or a heart. More usually a bunch of straw was tied up once so that the top spread out. Or a corn dolly, approaching closest to the original idea of a representation of the Mother Goddess, was made as follows: a bunch of wheat straw was stripped of feather, a band tied tightly round, four inches above that another band was tied, and the straw allowed to spring out, making a kind of body. It was tied again about three inches above that making a head, leaving the top to open out and be rounded off with shears.

Like ploughing, stacks were admired and criticized on Sunday morning walks. 'That's a tidy stack,' was said, 'but you want to go and see so-and-so's.' 'I remember one neighbour. No one could touch him building and thatching a stack. You'd think it had been shaved. One six yards long took him two days to thatch one side with either seaves or straw every one of them straight.'[1] Coconut fibre bands eventually superseded straw ropes, and the whole practice died out in the 1930s.

The custom of gleaning, threatened when horse rakes were introduced, faded out about the turn of the century. The corn gleaned from fields and hedgerows had been an essential addition to the economy of the cottager. 'I remember old John Metcalfe, his wife and family at Barugh [in the Vale of Pickering] who gathered as much wheat and barley as would make them flour for the winter and

[1] Mr H. Featherstone, Bilsdale.

meal for a pig. The farmer threshed it out for them. A lot of us lads went gleaning.'[1] 'My mother [who died in 1966 aged ninety-nine] used to go gleaning. She picked up the heads into a big sack-like pocket in her apron, then transferred them to bags. Dad flailed it.'[2] 'I've seen ten to twenty women in a field, mostly cookeepers from the town pastures. After flailing, four people holding the corners of a clean sheet threw it up and the *caff* [chaff] blew away.'[3]

Like gleaning, the great celebration of the Mell held at the end of leading was vanishing at the turn of the century. Richard Blakeborough then recollecting these events writes of the supper in the barn, the dancing and singing round the Mell Doll, and the performance of the Mell Act, a play handed down from generation to generation, or sometimes composed anew. The rhyme, with variations, shouted or sung ran:

> *Well bun an' better shorn,*
> *Is Mister [X's] corn.*
> *We hev her, we hev her*
> *As fast as a feather*
> *Hip! Hip! Hip! Hurrah! Hurrah!*

At Levisham it is recorded by B. M. Walker in *The Well of Life*, 1939, that about 1900 the corn dolly or harvest queen or corn baby was held high on a pole decorated with grain and flowers, and brought in from the fields accompanied by the shouting and singing of the harvesters. Later the pole with the dolly was reared up in the stackyard for the birds in winter.

The corn dolly was made similar in shape to the straw dozzle just described. Today the making of corn dollies, quite separated from the ancient custom, has developed into an interesting branch of folk art (*see plate* 187). However, mell suppers, held the night after the harvest was finished, are remembered. 'All is safely gathered in' was generally sung at the supper table which, laden with beef and ham, mell and curd cakes, might be decorated with a jug containing stalks of corn.

[1] Mr E. Mortimer, Pickering.
[2] Misses L. and A. Wilson, Wombleton.
[3] Mr I. Ventress, Wombleton.

THRESHING

OVER a comparatively short period, about 130 years, threshing has progressed from flailing to the horse wheel and barn thresher, to the steam engine and threshing machine, and lastly to the combine harvester. Side by side with these inventions the flail continued to be used on small moorland farms up to the 1930s and in one instance until 1967 (*see plates* 113–15), so that many people remember the process and the 'even steady and poetical sound of the thresher's flail' sounding in a village at night.[1]

The flail, often pronounced 'frail', the stick-and-a-half as it was called, consisted of the handstaff made of ash or willow about 54 inches long tapering from $1\frac{1}{8}$ inches to $\frac{3}{4}$ inch, topped by an iron loop, and the *swipple* made of holly or hazel, about 32 inches long or nine 'hands' (the width of a fist), fitted with a leather cap secured by two wooden pegs. The joint holding the two together by the loop and the cap was a narrow strip of leather about 8 inches long, or a length of *swarth* (skin) from a pig's chine, or a pig's *pissle* (penis). Whichever was used a slit was made at either end; one end was pushed through one slit and a wooden wedge inserted in the other[2] (*see drawings on page* 56). Flails were often home-made; or joiners provided the staff, and saddlers and blacksmiths the caps. In 1834 William Milner, blacksmith of Glaisdale, made '1 handstaff caping' for Jonathan Mary for 4*d.* (*see also plate* 112).[3]

Recollections have been handed down of flail men walking for miles, journeying round the Vale of Pickering all winter, perhaps staying a week on a farm.[4] Best reminds us that the old word for thresh was *bury*, and tells us that besides their pay men hired to flail had a threave of straw allowed each week, supposedly to buy and furnish them with swipples and 'flailebands' (a threave equalled two stooks or twenty-four sheaves).

[1] J. W. Ord, *History and Antiquities of Cleveland*, 1846.
[2] Mr B. Weatherill, Whitby, Mr F. Ward, East Moors, Mr F. Dowson, Rosedale, and Mr Jim Ainsley, Helmsley.
[3] Account book lent by Mr G. Lyth, Lealholm.
[4] Mr A. Watson, Kirkbymoorside.

The word bury appears in the couplet connected with the story of the hob of Hart Hall, Glaisdale, recorded by Canon Atkinson. Hob dressed in a ragged *sark* (shirt) used to flail at night for the farmer, but when he was given a *hardin hamp* (a smock-frock made of coarse hempen material) he was offended and said:

> *Gin Hob mun hae nowght but a hardin' hamp,*
> *He'll coom nae mair, nowther to berry nor stamp.*

Stamp refers to the process of *fautering* barley, that is knocking off the awms with a barley humbler (*see drawing on page* 56).[1]

In the eighteenth century both oats and rape were threshed in the open, and a public rape threshing was described by Marshall as 'one of the most striking scenes which occur in the field of Rural Economy'. He continued: 'If the quantity to be thrashed be large; as twenty to thirty acres; the whole country for many miles around, are collected. . . . Armies under engagement can scarcely exhibit, to general appearance, greater tumult; nor, on the parade, can they boast of better discipline. . . . The thrashers move continually in this ring; marching with slow step in pairs and in two divisions . . . with flails nimbly brandishing'[2] (*see plate* III.)

Joseph Ford also recalls that threshing days similar to ploughing days used to be great events, and that the last in Eskdale occurred at Houlsyke about 1836 when sixteen men and youths assembled to help a farmer who had moved and had extra corn stacks to thresh. Pieces of old ships' sails spread in a field made a threshing floor.

Dependent on the acreage of the farm and the area of the threshing floor, descriptions of flailing vary. Usually but not always the floor was a boarded section, perhaps 8 feet by 6 feet, or 9 feet by 10 feet, or 15 feet by 8 feet, sited in the barn between doors in either wall, the 'thruff duers' (through doors) opened for winnowing. On a stone floor two sheaves were set down and another, the one which was batted, laid across on top, the object being to protect the flail and not to crush the corn. Other people put four, six or twelve sheaves with their bands loosed and their heads meeting and overlapping in the middle. Some flailed before the bands were cut. If two were flailing they stood opposite each other and took alternate batts, keeping an even 'tip, tap, toe like a clock ticking'. If one fell out of step, he was liable to catch his head with the flail.

The flail was held loosely, especially by the left hand. 'You must let the stick turn in your hands all the time. You have to turn it to fetch it down flat.' 'The

[1] Rev. J. C. Atkinson, *Forty Years in a Moorland Parish* (1891), 1923 edition, p. 55.
[2] Marshall, *Rural Economy*, vol. II, pp. 22–35, 36–40, 1788.

staff was polished like glass in your hand.' 'It worked perfectly without going too high.' After one side had been batted, the sheaves were turned over (*see plate* 115), shaken, and the other sides were threshed. When a pile of corn about a foot high had accumulated, the straw was raked off, and two sheaves, sometimes three, were tied up with two bands to make a 'foddering'. For the upper band a bit of straw was drawn off and twisted under and round.[1] A bundle of straw was often called a *faud*, meaning as much as could be carried under an arm folded across the body.

Every winter's night after milking, up to nine o'clock or nine-thirty, enough corn for the next day was threshed, and if the farmer was going away for a day or on Saturdays to prepare for Sundays, two days' supplies were made ready. In snowy or wet weather flailing was a usual task. 'Mi father used to send me and my brother into t' barn to flail. I've brokken it dozens of times to get away from it.'[2] Mostly this was a man's job, but women took it on especially in emergencies. 'You had to do anything in those days.'[3]

The old method of *windering* (winnowing) was to open the through doors, fill a riddle and, standing on a box or stool, let the corn fall down and the caff blow away. Or if there was a trap door above, the corn could be dropped from a height, or men taking handfuls or armed with wooden shovels threw the corn into the air. Winnowing machines, often made locally and worked by hand, were however common (*see plate* 116).

The horse wheel, providing power to drive a threshing machine, was introduced into the North Riding by E. Cleaver of Nunnington in lower Ryedale in 1790. Supplied by Rastrick of Morpeth, Co. Durham, it cost about £100.[4] But these did not reach the dales until the 1820s. One was installed at Whitethorn Farm, Cropton, in 1825, and the first in Danbydale at Stormy Hall in 1830.[5]

There were two types, spoken of as fixtures and portables, of which the former were the earlier. The principle employed for both was that horses walking round and round at their normal pace of four miles an hour turned gear wheels con-

---

[1] Mr F. Ward, Old Kiln, East Moors, Mr F. Grayson, Sleights, formerly of Lease Rigg, Grosmont, Mr Jim Ainsley, Helmsley, formerly of Bilsdale, Mr B. Tyreman, Newgate Foot, Pockley, Mr B. Weatherill, Whitby.

[2] Mr H. Peirson, Hartoft.

[3] Mrs W. D. Smith, Newton-on-Rawcliffe, formerly of Hartoft.

[4] J. W. Ord, *History and Antiquities of Cleveland*, 1846. See also A. and J. K. Harrison, 'The Horse Wheel in North Yorkshire', *Bulletin of Cleveland and Teesside Local History Society*, no. 8, March 1970; and F. Atkinson, 'The Horse as a Source of Rotary Power', *Newcomen Society*, vol. XXXIII, 1960–61.

[5] See beam with date at Ryedale Folk Museum, and Joseph Ford, *Some Reminiscences and Folk Lore of Danby Parish and District*, 1953.

111. *A public rape threshing possibly in the Vale of Pickering; from Walker's* Costume of Yorkshire (*1814*). *The threshers worked in pairs with two going backwards and the next two forwards and so on.*

THE FLAIL

112. *Mr Paul Atkinson, Rose Cottage, Goathland, with a flail. He was a greengrocer who helped out on farms* (c. *1911*).

113. *Mr F. Ward, Old Kiln, East Moors, who grew a small quantity of corn, and used a flail up to 1967. The flail staff is held lightly and twisted.*

114. *The swipple falls flat on the heads of corn.*

FLAILING AND WINNOWING

115. *The sheaves are turned in the manner shown with staff and foot.*

116. *Mr Garbutt Agar, North Ghyll, Farndale, demonstrates using a winnowing machine.*

117. *Mr J. Lumsden, Rawson Syke, Farndale, using a horse wheel. One, made by Tinsley, was installed here about 1865. This was moved from Tenter Hill, Farndale, and has four starts for four horses. Note the tumbling shaft running towards the door at ground level, and the opening above for communication between driver and the person feeding sheaves into the thresher inside the barn (c. 1933).*

HORSE WHEELS

118. *Wheel shed at Mountain Ash Farm, Glaisdale.*

119. *The structure of an indoor wheel partially complete at Drummer Hill Farm, near Ingleby Greenhow. It has four starts; the large wheel was on top of the framework and the whole rotated on the spindle in the stone base.*

120. *Mr R. M. Pearson and Robert Pickering demonstrate feeding sheaves into a barn thresher formerly used with a three-horse portable horse wheel.*

121. *Large barn thresher powered by a horse wheel at Frost Hall, Farndale. This both threshed and winnowed. The fan for winnowing was contained in the cylinder underneath and shakers carried the straw to eject it on the right.*

THRESHING AND GRINDING

122. *Grinding mill made by J. Weighell, Albert Foundry, Pickering. It was powered by the horse wheel.*

123. *Mr K. Storey with the grinding mill which was worked by water power and a water wheel at Underpark Farm, Lealholm.*

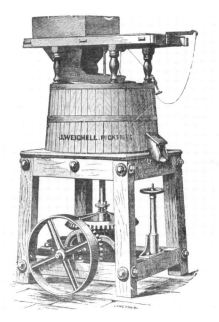

nected to the threshing machine by a tumbling (driving) shaft, and so were able to raise the speed of the drum of the thresher to some 800 revolutions per minute.

For the fixtures, stone-built wheel sheds, adjuncts to the farm buildings, housed the horse walk or trod, also the gearing and structure for from four to six horses. Sometimes square, sometimes five- or six-sided, wheel sheds measured internally about 27 feet by 27 feet. From eaves to eaves across the centre a massive beam supported a central shaft, the overhead starts (beams), and the wheel above nine to ten feet in diameter, cast in segments. The earliest had wooden central shafts, tumbling shafts and cogs made of hornbeam.

Although the machinery in them has gone, wheel sheds may be seen on farms between Stokesley and Kildale, at Stormy Hall, Danbydale, Postgate and Mountain Ash, Glaisdale, Stonebeck Gate, Little Fryup, Fryup Hall, Head House and Ajalon House, Great Fryup, at Frost Hall, Head House and Monket House, Farndale; and, complete with machinery, one from Urra Farm, Bilsdale, at the Ryedale Folk Museum. Another at Drummer Hill Farm, near Ingleby Greenhow, outside our area, also retains part of the original structure (*see plate* 119).

The horses were led in at different doors or, entering at one door, they followed each other round to take up their positions. They wore *barfins* (collars) and head collars or halters tied to rings on the framework and were yoked by chains (as if to cart shafts) to lengths of wood bolted to the ends of the starts. Sometimes all of them, sometimes two, wore cart saddles and breechings for the purpose of stopping the wheel when ordered. Attended by a boy or a girl walking in the middle in the opposite direction to the horses, they worked for a morning or about two hours perhaps once a week or once a fortnight threshing out a pike. Often the children helped for an hour before going to school. In the barn a man fed the sheaves into the threshing machine, a woman handed them to him, another man tied and made straw bands and another put away. It was hot work for the horses, hence the open sides of many sheds; and at Drummer Hill salt and water were always prepared in readiness to wash them down.[1]

Because of the clumsy gears horse wheels rattled loudly. They were regarded as a means of breaking in a young horse which, working with three older ones in a four-horse wheel, was led by a halter, with a rope looped round its body from the top of the start so that it couldn't lie down.[2] Sometimes when unused to the work, horses became dizzy and had to be rested. Very occasionally they were trapped and killed or because of a yoke being unfastened broke their necks.[3] Yet

[1] Miss M. K. Shotton, Drummer Hill.
[2] Mr F. Raw, Ainthorpe.
[3] Mr A. Douks, Kirkbymoorside.

noisy, monotonous and sometimes dangerous as the work might seem, horses, liking company, enjoyed it and when loosed out from ploughing were known to make straight for the wheel shed.[1]

The portables, so called because the whole outfit might be transported on a farm waggon with two horses, consisted of wheels, shaft and starts for from one to four horses fixed to an oak framework on the ground in the open outside a barn with the thresher inside. Sometimes the tumbling shaft was let into a channel, sometimes the horses had actually to step over it. A seat on the start for a man or boy keeping an eye on the horses, inspired the description of a hired man as 'too idle to sit up on a start'.

Advertised and made at local foundries in the 1850s, many date from that period (*see plates* 70 *and* 117). Whilst few farms had fixtures, only five for instance in Rosedale, most had a portable. John Tinsley of Farndale, who made barn threshers almost entirely of wood and bought the necessary castings for the wheels from Carter's foundry, hired them out, and if someone bought one, made another. Sometimes the thresher was shared, as it was between Head House and North Ghyll, Farndale, and transported by horses from one farm to the other. The horse walk at Hollins, Farndale, has a striking high walled platform built up to accommodate it.

Mr W. W. Featherstone relates that when his grandfather was living at Elm House at the head of Farndale, he bought from Weighell's of Pickering a portable wheel and thresher that was delivered on a waggon. The first time it was used the horses ran away and as a result the wooden cogs of the wheels were broken. His grandfather had to go by horse and cart to Pickering fourteen miles away to fetch the millwright who returned with him and stayed three days mending the cogs.

Usually the fixtures had combined threshing and winnowing machines, although these came later, whilst the portables only worked small threshers (*see plates* 120, 121). In the latter the corn passed through riddles and flailing was simulated by iron and wood beaters fixed on a drum that rotated inside the concave (outer casing). When fixing them the distance between the beaters and the concave was gauged by a clenched fist and at the bottom where it narrowed by outstretched fingers.[2]

Small engines and old motor cars began to replace horses in the 1920s although horse wheels were used at Postgate and Mountain Ash, Glaisdale, and Head House, Great Fryup until the early 1940s.

[1] Mr W. L. Thompson, Glaisdale.
[2] Mr E. Benson, Ruswarp, whose family, plough makers and millwrights, set up many portables of different sizes, the last at Abbot's House, Goathland, for the Smailes family.

In Rosedale another form of horse power, the paddling machine built in a paddle house, has been described to us by Mr F. Dowson, of Rosedale. There were three in the dale at Gill Bank, Newlands, and Thorgill Farms, and for them a small cart mare of about fifteen hands was employed to paddle a metal wheel about eighteen inches wide with wooden slats, half sunk in the ground.

The mare approached the paddle house, a small building like a stall with splayed boarded sides, up a gently sloping plank, and attached by chains from its collar to the sides, it then walked in the same place slightly uphill treading the wheel backwards for about an hour at a time. A tumbling shaft was attached to the wheel and a hand lever braked and stopped it. As much corn could be threshed in this way as by any other means; in fact the one at Thorgill was replaced by a three-horse thresher to no advantage. That at Gill Bank, the last to be worked, ceased to be used about 1920.

Threshing sets, that is six- to seven-horsepower steam engines and large threshing machines on wheels, added to later by straw trussers, although in use in the neighbourhood by the 1850s onwards,[1] did not begin to replace horse wheels in the dales until the first decade of this century.

The first engines, called portables, lacked traction power and drove only the threshing machine, and were fitted with double shafts and drawn from farm to farm by a team of six horses. The horses first took the engine and then returned for the machine. Sometimes up hills in the Wolds twenty were necessary (*see plate* 130). Experiences in the snow, of machines toppling over hedges out of control, resulted in farmers on large farms buying their own sets. The story goes of a team failing to breast a hill, when a menagerie came by, and the help of an elephant was enlisted to push the engine up with its head. When the first engine came to Kirkbymoorside about the turn of the century all the town turned out to see it.

Threshing began as soon as harvest was over, even before, but generally about 24th September, and it went on until 't' spring o' t' year'. 'Everyone wanted you together, but once you had been round it was better.' Mostly different firms travelling with sets and charging within recollection £4 a day served their own areas. Watson Garbutt of Seamer is remembered as the largest with twelve sets or more; Yates had nine, including five Ransome engines, two Marshall, one Fowler and one Aveling and Porter. Wood and Whites of Harome had three; Thackrays of Brawby two; Russells of Edstone had two, and Russells of Kirkbymoorside took their 'steamer' up Rosedale; there were Charley Turner of Lazenby, near

---

[1] *Malton Messenger*, 6th October 1855.

Eston, and Harry Beeforth of Hawsker serving Eskdale, and others based on Lythe and Hinderwell.

Farms of different sizes had so many threshing days. Skiplam Grange had twenty-three. Some arranged for one day a month, and small farms in the dales might have only half to one day a year and even less. A staff of twelve or fourteen men was required of which the firm provided three men; the engine driver, who about 1920 earned 10s. a day, his mate the steersman who fed sheaves into the machine, and the flagman, who had originally walked in front carrying a flag to warn approaching drivers and hold their horses. Paid by the farmer, he cut the bands of the sheaves.

The farmer supplied the rest: forkers, corn carriers, builders of stacks, and the knockabout, often the farmer himself, who attended to odd jobs and the supply of water for the engine. He also laid in a barrel of beer bought at 1s. a gallon. On the Wolds the tramp threshers or Wold rangers followed on from farm to farm earning 2s. 6d. a day, but in the dales where neighbours helped neighbours it was all 'borrowed labour'. Corn carriers on account of the heavy work earned 7s. a day, and feats of strength were sometimes recorded on granary walls, for instance, the carrying up the steps of a sack of peas weighing thirty-four stones. Eighty quarters of barley (thirty-two stones to the quarter), forty to fifty quarters of wheat (thirty-six stones to the quarter) and up to 100 quarters of oats (twenty-four stones to the quarter) could be threshed in a big day on a farm on good land.

Mr E. Mortimer of Pickering, who started in 1919 driving the engine of a threshing set for Yates of Malton in the Pickering area, has described to us the routine and some of his experiences. The dates of the threshing days had been arranged beforehand with the farmers. Travelling at about four miles an hour and carrying three or four hundredweight of best quality coal and a tank of water, the set was moved on as arranged from farm to farm.

On a Monday morning when the engine was cold, Ernest Mortimer had to be back at the farm at 5 a.m. to fire the engine, and get up steam. Ordinarily throughout the week the fire, damped down by putting a lid on the chimney, stayed in all night so that a 7 a.m. start was usual. The engine was oiled, the belt put on, the whistle blown and 'away you went hell for leather until 5 p.m.' ''Lowance time [drinkings] when the engine was oiled again was 10 a.m., dinner at midday, 'lowance again at 3 p.m. or 3.30.' At 5 they packed up and moved on, with two hurricane lamps in front and a red one behind, to the next farm, had tea and supper, then cycled home. Older hands used to stay on the farm. One used to go to Sledmere on the Wolds and walked home twelve miles on a Saturday, returned on Monday morning, all for a gold sovereign a week.

Difficulties were often experienced at night in the dark manœuvring up farm lanes or into stackyards where it was 'all puddle and muck', and frequently grabs, angle bars, eight in all, had to be fitted to each big back wheel, in which there were holes to insert bolts for fixing them. The engine had a drum holding fifty yards of rope which was sometimes used to drag the threshing machine into position. The big wheels could also be fitted with frost pins. Ernest Mortimer's father once turned completely round in the snow and found himself going in the opposite direction. Nor was threshing without danger. Hands were hurt and arms broken, and because a man could overbalance into the drum, feeding in sheaves was hazardous work.

Farmers themselves remember the huge quantities of food required for a threshing day and the succulence of one and a half stones of 'threshing meat'. Most farmers' wives provided an abundance; a few were mean or incompetent so that 'we had to tak wi own'.

Ernest Mortimer remembers one farm in particular nicknamed Rabbit Pie Hall because he and the workers were once given a pie containing thirteen rabbit heads. They ate the pastry and gravy. This place provided two-pronged forks and knives sharpened down to stumps, so that when offered watery rice pudding they tipped up their plates and drank it. Sometimes cakes were so hard that it was suggested they be used for grabs, and that the lard was 'out o' t' pump'. Again on a farm on the Wolds, where food was usually rough but good, they sat at a huge table in the farm kitchen, and the foreman carving great lumps off the joint flipped a piece in turn, landing it exactly on each plate all down the long table. As we have said, on the small dale farms the men eating with the family fared better.

Yates of Malton sold all their threshing sets for £7,000 to £8,000 in 1944 and with the proceeds bought combine harvesters. Although a few people still cut corn with a self-binder and assemble a team of men for a threshing day, each year the number dwindles and the combine, either owned outright or hired from a contractor, takes over.

124. *Mr H. Worley, Lamplands Farm, Egton, with an Albion Swathe turner, pulled by Violet, aged seventeen, a Clydesdale.*

125. *Mr J. Jackson, and Polly, Stonegate, Lealholm, using a horse rake by Mattison of Bedale in the Bigger Meadow.*

126. *Mr H. Worley, Lamplands Farm, Egton, using a* mannishment *fertilizer (drill) made by Massey-Harris for basic slag, nitrogen etc.*

FENCES   127. *Members of the Danby and District Young Farmers' Club building a wall at Danby Village Hall (1959).*

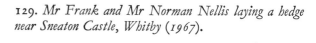

128. *Mr J. M. Lister, Glaisdale, finishing laying a hedge.*

129. *Mr Frank and Mr Norman Nellis laying a hedge near Sneaton Castle, Whitby (1967).*

130. *A threshing machine ready to be drawn by a shaft horse and six pairs of horses at Burdale House, near Wharram-le-Street, Yorkshire Wolds (1911).*

THRESHING

131. *Threshing with a horse-drawn (portable) engine and threshing machine at Wilton near Pickering. Members of the Armstrong family, and the farmer, John Armstrong, on the left (1896).*

132. *A threshing day at Tape Barn, Swainsey Lane, Pickering. The farmer, C. Ellis, is standing on the stack, and the engine driver is Mr Ernest Mortimer. The set is a Marshall's of Gainsborough with a 6 h.p. steam engine, no. 19500, introduced about 1875 (1913).*

133. *Threshing day at the Listers at Tofts Farm, Pickering. A Marshall's set, engine no. 31092, owned by Yates of Malton. The tank on the left holds water (1936).*

134. *Threshing machine driven by a tractor at Oxclose Farm, Hutton-le-Hole. William Hall, Robert Davison, H. Stead, T. Frank and others (1948).*

THRESHING

135. *Threshing day at Mr L. Frank's, Underhill Farm, Farndale. The Garvie machine is being run by a tractor, with a team of ten men—two on the rick, one feeding in sheaves, three dealing with sacks, two men leading the corn, one raking up chaff, and one making a new stack with bracken for a base.*

136. 'Lowance time at a threshing day at Oxclose Farm, Hutton-le-Hole (1948).

DAYS

137. 'Lowance time during the harvest on Lund Court Farm, near Kirkbymoorside in 1970. John Pickard, Ernest Pearson and R. Biggins.

DRESSING A MILLSTONE

138. *Mr A. Robinson, former miller of Rievaulx, having rubbed off the millstone with a hard stone, is proving it with the staff smeared with red rudd.*

139. *The furrows, which must be the correct depth, are ruled by a feather dipped in rudd or ink and water and measured out by two lathes, known as the furrow spline and the land spline.*

140. *Dressing a furrow with a mill bill (a pick). The furrow has a straight and a sloping side.*

141. *Dressing a furrow using a mill bill with a chisel.*

142. *Finishing the top stone by giving it 'swallow'.*

144. *Ugthorpe Mill, which ceased to work in 1911.*

△

143. *Rievaulx Mill before it was raised another story about 1870. It ceased to be worked in 1961.*

145. *Levisham Mill wheel put in by Mr Henry Benson (in the billycock hat), of Ruswarp. The castings were made by Hutton's Foundry, Whitby, from patterns supplied by the Bensons (1904).*

146. *Bransdale Mill. The initials 'W. S.' (the wall-ties) stand for William Strickland.*

CORN MILLS

PEAT AND TURF

THE quiet of the moorlands today belies their usefulness in the past. They yielded, and still do in a small way, many products that were essential to subsistence in the valleys. On the moors peat and turf were cut for *eldin* (fuel); ling was pulled for kindling, thatching, and besom making; bracken and seaves were harvested for thatching and bedding for stock; bilberries, cranberries and whortleberries were gathered, and sphagnum moss collected for dressing wounds in war time and for nurserymen for wrapping plants at the present day.

The open moors—Spaunton, Danby, Glaisdale, Egton, Wheeldale, Goathland, Fylingdales and others—form the commons of individual manors whose boundaries, often in dispute, used regularly to be ridden. Both freeholders and cottagers possessed common rights vested in the older houses, and leases of farms and land included rights of common of pasture, turbary, peats, stones, 'breckons', ling and sometimes furze. Those without rights paid 'turfgraste' for *graving* turves, as small sums may still be paid for getting peat or turf, although not under that name.

Rights of turbary appear frequently in monastic charters and peat and turf were dug in many more places than would appear possible now, including the Carrs of the Vale of Pickering almost to the coast near Filey. Until the seventeenth century fuel used at Scarborough was mostly peat got from the moorlands north of it and from the extensive Allerston Moor near Pickering.[1] Special areas were sometimes allotted on the moors for the use of the tenants of a manor, and the sale of peat and turf, regulated by manor courts, often caused trouble and ill feeling. From the fourteenth to the nineteenth century records show that this occasionally took the form of the throwing down and burning of the stacks drying 'remote from Company in the wide Moors'.[2]

For the graving of peat and turf entirely different tools and techniques were employed. Peat was cut from deep bogs, whilst turf was pared from the surface

---

[1] J. B. Barker, *History of Scarborough*, 1882.
[2] *The Honor and Forest of Pickering*, vol. III, 1896, ed. R. B. Turton, NRRS; NRRO, ZF 7/16/1; and Poster at Beck Isle Museum, Pickering.

of the moor. Turf, more easily procured than peat, dried more quickly, did not shrink, and because of the sand in it burnt both brighter and hotter. Yet peat dug from bogs did not devastate the moors, and people journeyed several miles to peat holes. However, proximity to one source or the other determined which kind was dug.

Peat is found in two types of bog—the first in the valleys in wet slacks (hollows) which originated from the melt-water channels of glaciers, such as Randy Mere and others round about Goathland. In the second kind of bog, peat was formed over the centuries largely from sphagnum moss, and it blankets the watershed of the rivers Derwent and Esk at over 1,000 feet above sea level. Elsewhere there were many other bogs.

Methods of cutting and drying peat vary slightly from district to district. At Goathland they went *kenning* and made *kens*[1] (conical heaps perhaps so named from the shape, which resembled a plunger churn), which were 4 to 5 feet high built up like open brickwork. Although most of these valley peat bogs are abandoned or planted with trees, Randy Mere on the road to Egton Bridge was in use in 1971.

Easily within living memory the bogs of the moorland heights—Fryup, Bluewath or Glaisdale Head, Pike Hill and Wintergill on Egton High Moor, also Black Pits on Wheeldale Moor—were alive with people from Danbydale, Fryup, Glaisdale, Egton, Delves and elsewhere in peat-cutting time in the spring. 'We liked to go up in a company' and after a hard day's work 'there was a proper stream of traffic on a night, all horses'.

The workings near Bluewath Beck, some old, some still used, are conveniently reached by several peat roads branching off from the moorland road between Glaisdale and Rosedale, and stretch from the head waters of the beck rising on Cock Heads almost a mile downstream. In places the faces of the peat holes are 10 feet high, worked in two tiers. When Mr F. Macdonald of Fryup started to cut peat here in 1927, the face was alongside the beck, but by annual cuttings (usually two across a breast, amounting to a depth of 2 feet 6 inches) it has receded fifty-five yards southwards. A generation before that it was on the north side of the beck.

The face is here called the breast and each man has a hole 7 to 9 feet across and from 6 to 10 feet deep—a size which allowed two men to cut a *dess* in a day, that is a spit across from top to bottom. The first time the peat cutter goes up, he shaves off 6 inches of the full front of the breast, the frost layer, and spreads the waste peat level at the foot, leaving a narrow drainage channel. Next with a hay

[1] F. W. Dowson, *Goathland in History and Folk-Lore*, 1947; also Mr T. W. Ventress, Egton.

or an ordinary spade he nicks down the back about 18 inches from the face and pares off a layer from the top. 'Nicking the backside is one o' t' main jobs, and it wants to have a battered back [a slight slope].'

The cutter, standing at the bottom of the peat hole, on a sod if the face is high to start with, proceeds to cut (*see plates* 147–8). Peat spades, with a wing on one side or the other depending on the use by a right-handed or a left-handed person,[1] were similar on both sides of the moorlands except for some with a little more style (*see drawing on page* 78). In the spade depicted the iron is nicely shaped at the back, whereas most had straight pieces of metal. Each peat, 15 inches to 18 inches long by 5 inches wide and 4 inches thick, was cast straight from the spade on to the barrow, and by pressing on them as you drew the spade away, you *sliped* them, thus putting a glaze on that withstood water. A well-dried peat could be immersed in water and turn the wet.[2] It was possible to cut 2,000 peats 18 inches long in a day.[3]

Next, the peats are barrowed to the *ligging* ground—a comparatively new idea.[4] Formerly they were carried in scuttles made of willow or on a special *gripe* (fork) three at a time for a man and two for a woman.[5] Now two barrows, one being filled and the other being wheeled to the ligging ground, are usual. The women always helped with peat getting, especially with the next process of setting up, and Mr and Mrs J. Underwood (*seen on plates* 147–9) formed a typical family team.

After a week or so the peats were turned over or set in threes by leaning two against one laid on edge. Latterly this process was omitted. Usually peats were *rickled* (heaped) in Bransdale by propping one up in the centre and arranging others round it with the glazed side outwards, but at Bluewath the rickles of eight to sixteen peats are built up in twos like children's bricks with one on top (*see plate* 150).

After haytime, leading at Bluewath began by lifting whole rickles all but the two bottom peats and carrying them to waggon or sledge, or if they had to be taken some distance a *hicking* (hand) barrow was used. Finally the bottoms—the two left—are rickled and led a few days later. The bodies of waggons were filled, then peats were laid carefully in courses, and the whole roped round with sacks at the corners (*see plate* 152).

[1] Mr R. Foord, Wild Slack, Lealholm.
[2] Mr H. Bentley, Pickering, formerly of Bransdale.
[3] Mr J. Jackson, Low Hollins Farm, Egton Bridge.
[4] Mr J. Underwood, Ainthorpe.
[5] Mr W. L. Thompson, Glaisdale.

Mr R. Welford of Glaisdale remembered as a boy of eight or nine walking eight miles to Pike Hill with a rhubarb and date pie and a can of tea for his father working there, whilst Mrs T. Cornforth, then living at Mountain Ash, Glaisdale, describes how about thirty-five years ago they took food for the day and were a week cutting at Wintergill and a week leading. They always got twenty loads of peat and never burnt any other fuel. 'Good peat won't bear the frost, but it dries quicker.' 'You want black peat; it's the nearest thing to coal.' But nowadays it is said that the cost of getting it is 'woss than the cost of buying coal', and in 1971, depending on whether they had time in the spring, only six or eight families went to Bluewath.

The deepest peat deposits to be worked are on Peat Bog Moor formerly on the Hackness Estate near the Falcon Inn off the Scarborough to Whitby road. Here all the tenants of the estate had right of turbary. Great numbers of people cut and rickled throughout the summer from April to July. 'It was like a fair.' The breast was 21 feet high, worked in three desses (here in stepped tiers), so that from the top, eight or twelve peats 11 inches long by 6 inches thick had to be barrowed down on heavy planks to the middle tier and then to ground level. 'It was one of the hardest jobs I've ever done.'[1]

Each farm had a 'floor' for setting the peats about 3 yards by 10 yards wide with ditches in between. So many square yards of flooring were required for a waggon load and usually a farm with five or six men cut eighteen loads. When backing the waggons up to the floor for leading, there was the danger of the horses sinking in up to their bellies.

Here men used also to be employed all summer cutting peat. Their spades, kept bright and as sharp as a razor, lasted only two seasons. They either worked by 'tak', that is 10s. for a ten-course load, or were paid £1 a week, finding their own meat. It used to be said that 1,000 peats made a cart load.[2] At the present day the bog, situated in the midst of trees planted by the Forestry Commission, is not as as deep as it was and is confined to one acre. In 1970 about six men were working here, paying 1s. for the privilege.

Turf cutting began with the burning of a *swithen*, *swizzen*, or *swidden* in March before the grouse nested, often under the supervision of a gamekeeper (*see plate* 154). It was usually undertaken the year before cutting, or a swizzen burnt about ten years earlier might be chosen because a two or three years' growth of ling was liked. Burnt to keep the moor in condition, a swizzen might cover ten to forty acres. For turf 'we would grave each year about a quarter the size of Helmsley

[1] Mr E. W. Nesfield, High Langdale End, Harwooddale.
[2] Mr G. Allanson, Harwooddale and Mr T. Knaggs, Harwooddale.

market-place',[1] and this was marked and claimed by an initial carved out of the sod in two or three places—a centuries' old practice, specified in 1682 by the manor court of Fylingdales[2] (*see plate* 162). The burnt moor looked 'like a quilt that had been worked'.

Taking note of the direction of the wind two or more men and boys kept the fire under control with various types of beaters. But care had to be exercised, for the history of the moors is punctuated with disastrous fires. A stone dated 13th March 1893 on Lealholm Rigg marks the place where Willie Shaw, aged eighty-nine, having gone up to burn a swizzen, lost control of the fire and was burnt to death.

Formerly burnt heather stems—ling *cowls* or *gowldans* or *gooldens*—were pulled for a supply of kindling for the year (*see plates* 155–6). Bundles, tied up with ling bands or twine, were rolled down steep hillsides towards the farmhouses, carried over the shoulder across slacks, or led loose on sledges. A bundle of good thick cowls lasted two months, and careful families tied them up into little parcels ready for putting on the fire. Stanley Umpleby, dialect poet, gave the title of one of his poems, 'A Bo'ddin [burden] o' Cowls' to a volume of his poetry.[3] Another poem is called 'Torfin Taame', and in a third he wrote of the men and boys singing, 'Awaay ower t' moors bo'nnin' swiddens o' ling'.

The tools required were turf spades and *knappers* (*see drawings page* 78). Of these, variations were the cock and hen spades, which differed in the blade. The cock, the most common, has one wing turned up at a right angle, and the hen has two turned up in a curve at each side. Thus the first slices two sides of a turf, and the second three. The hen spade, which we have seen only in Goathland and the moorlands round Whitby, proved useful for cutting small areas on a poor moor, and also it was possible with it to leave narrow strips of ling to grow up again in between the graving.

Besides the blades, handles varied. The belly spade, again the most common, measured some 6 feet from the tip of the blade to the top of the handle, and was pushed from the loins. The shorter thigh or knee spade, about 5 feet overall, and straighter with a half handle for easy manoeuvrability, was pushed by the thighs or by the knees when it was used in a crouching position.[4]

For use with the first a man wore belly knappers hung round his waist, and for

[1] Mr Jim Ainsley, Helmsley, formerly of Bilsdale.
[2] NRRO, ZCG 111 1/1.
[3] Also in *A Cleveland Anthology*, ed. Bill Cowley, published by the Yorkshire Dialect Society, 1963.
[4] Mr J. Welford, Hinderwell, Mr H. Tindall, Danby; and notes of Mr J. Weatherill (1860–1960).

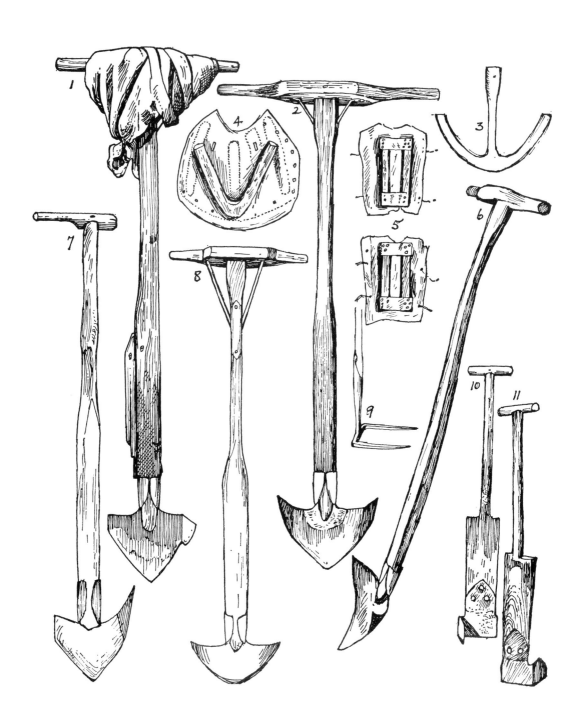

the second thigh knappers tied one to each leg above the knees. Knappers were made from pieces of leather, perhaps from an old saddle or the top of a *barfin* (horse collar) on to which a forked piece or strips of wood were fixed respectively. They might be padded behind with sacking.

Blacksmiths made both peat and turf spades. Mr W. Atkinson of Sneaton recalls being able to buy a *slipe* (strip) of shear steel 6 feet long by 1 foot wide, out of which seven or eight blades could be shaped. Blades made in Sheffield and Birmingham could also be bought at ironmongers' shops.

Joiners specialized in making shafts of *selly* (sallow), required to be as light as possible, and they sometimes used the forked branch of a tree so that the forks fitted into the handle. They always matched the length of the shaft and angle of the blade to the height of each man, who was asked 'Wheea's t' owd 'n?' to copy from. Shafts might be curved but were often straight so that the bend in the blade (a weak spot often strengthened by a patch of metal riveted on) gave the correct angle for cutting; or, especially to adjust the angle for the shorter thigh spade, pieces of leather were wedged between blade and shaft either at the back or the front.

If need be the blade could be knocked off and a sod spade put on for graving sods cut as long as possible for potato clamps. Mr J. Weatherill writes: 'At the turn of the century an old stalwart of the craft [of sod cutting] told me that he cut them by piece work at the rate of 1*s*. 1½*d*. for 100 and that he could grave 300 in a day. He commented that some little time before they had been "nobbut 1*s*. per 100", which was a bit tight, and he had had to work hard to make ends meet.' These sods gave excellent protection for clamps and lasted for two seasons.

With his spade over his shoulder the turf cutter started out for the moor. Arrived at his swidden he cut across the end of the strip he was to pare and then went back about two feet and *bucked* (pushed) his spade forward, turning the turf over as in ploughing. He then kept going back and repeating the process. Turf cuts best when wet, but even so on the first day stiffness and bruises resulted.

TURF AND PEAT SPADES

1 Cock spade (handle 5 feet 9 inches to tip of blade and width of blade 10 inches). 2 Hen spade (handle 5 feet 7 inches, blade 13 inches), made by W. Pennock, Goathland. 3 Turf spade at the Whitby Museum. 4 Knappers for use with the belly spade (R.F.M.). 5 Knappers for use with the thigh spade (R.F.M.). 6 Side view of 2. 7 Thigh spade, usually with a shorter shaft, with half handle. 8 Sod spade (handle 5 feet, blade 1 foot 1 inch) used for getting sods to cover potato pies. 9 Turf rake for dragging turves from turf stacks. 10 and 11 Front and back of peat spade to cut a peat 16 inches by 5 inches by 3 inches.

After that in a spell of fine weather a good man working hard might grave five or six waggon loads, that is about fifteen *rooks* (small stacks) in a day.

Turves may be set up at once two over one, laying one on its side and propping two up against it (*see plate* 160). Then if they were not quite dry and dare not be left, fireheaps were made by placing three or four turves upended in a circle with others piled round them.[1] Or *hipples* (heaps), which could be of peats or turves, built up like bricks were an intermediate stage.[2] But usually round or oblong rooks about 5 feet high were made in about a week's time in good weather. For these, turves were placed flat at the corners first one way then another, then those forming the sides were laid like bricks sometimes on edge sometimes flat, and the whole topped with a roof of turves overlapping like the slates of a house, finally capped by wettish turves laid across the ridge (*see plate* 161). One rook was reckoned to supply a week's fuel for one fire.

They were led after three or four weeks, perhaps half before clipping and half after haytime. Sledges held one and a half and waggons three rooks. When coming down the steep turf banks, the holloways or tracks still to be seen behind almost every farm in many dales especially Farndale, a back wheel of a waggon, or even both, were tied up with a *tame* (chain), or fitted with a special ridged shoe; or one was tied up and one shoe fitted. If the way was very steep a small loaded sledge was hitched behind to act as a brake. The load was carefully packed with turves laid flat in the waggon body and built up above as for making a turf stack (described next). Sacks were placed at the corners round each of which the waggon rope was looped and made fast.[3] Seven hundred turves made a waggon load, and for a moderate sized farm such as North Ghyll, Farndale, about twenty-five waggon loads used to be got each year.

Some farms had a turf house, but usually stacks, built in coupons (that is, in a close row), each perhaps 3 or 4 yards long by 3 yards wide[4]—some were huge—were built near to the house. First quoins were made of three turves laid flat first one way then the other until the required height was reached. Then they were placed layer by layer, slanting first one way then the other in herringbone formation with the long side of the turf facing the gable end and the ling side downwards. In between single courses a layer was laid flat, and at about the fifth or sixth course the stack was gradually built up in the shape of a roof as described in building rooks. 'When set like this they looked champion.' Formerly

[1] Mr G. Agar, North Ghyll, Farndale.
[2] Mr K. Eddon, Saddler House, Goathland.
[3] Mr H. Cook, formerly of Dale Head, Westerdale.
[4] Mr K. Eddon, Saddler House, Goathland.

they were thatched with ling. In July 1834 William Milner of Glaisdale charged
Joseph Collier 1s. for 'turf stacks thacking'.[1]

Many people using a stack made the previous year kept a year's supply of fuel
behind them. At Hamer House they had a three years' supply.[2] The construction
was designed to ease the work of pulling out turves from the gable end with a
drag (two-tined fork). Brought into the house in scuttles and skeps, the turves
made the famous turf fires already described.

Within recollection most houses in the dales burnt nothing but turf or peat.
They might have a hundredweight or two of coal for an occasional sitting-room
fire or for Christmas, or buy 'Threshing coal' for when the threshing set came
round. The scent of burning turf or peat permeating the villages was one of the
familiar features welcoming people home after the day's work or after a long
absence.

[1] Account book of William Milner, blacksmith, Glaisdale, lent by Mr G. Lyth, Lealholm.
[2] Mr J. M. Lister, Glaisdale.

PEAT CUTTING

147. *Mr and Mrs J. Underwood cutting peat at Fryup Peat Hole. They cut peat here for about ten years and during that time found the horn of a* Bos primigenius *and a jet button dating from about 1500* B.C.

148. *The peat is laid direct on to a barrow.*

149. *The peats are transferred from the barrow with a fork on to the drying ground.*

150. *Mr R. Welford builds a rickle, the next stage in the drying process, at Bluewath.*

151. *Mr R. Hugill, Mr J. Atkinson, and a boy leading turves by sledge down a turf bank, Farndale East Crag (1936).*

152. *The Cornforths, Mountain Ash Farm, Glaisdale, leading peat. They have stopped to remove the shoe on the 'drive' wheel of the waggon. Note sacks placed at each corner of the load (c. 1938).*

LEADING TURF AND PEAT

153. *Mr F. and Mr K. Macdonald, Bainleyside, Fryup, and helpers loading peat at Bluewath Beck, Glaisdale Head. The 'bottoms' of the rickles have been left for later collection. The straight peat face can be seen in the far distance.*

LING COWLS   154. *Burning a swidden on Spaunton Moor above Hutton-le-Hole. The moor fire is being controlled by Joe and Jackson Cole (1908).*

155. *Mr G. Thompson, South View, High Walls, Lealholm, with a 'boddin o' cowls' (a burden of burnt heather stems). One bundle of a good thickness provided two months' kindling.*

156. *Mrs J. W. Teasdale, Beestone Farm, Farndale, pulling ling cowls on Spaunton Moor.*

TURF CUTTING

157. *Mr George Collier, wearing knappers, cutting turf to make eighty rooks on Blakey Moor (1936).*

158. *Mr Jim Graham, Hunt House, Goathland, cutting turf on Goathland Moor, using a cock spade, and sacking instead of knappers.*

159. *When cut the requisite length, he turns the turf over.*

LING

LING (heather), besides being used for kindling as already described, provided thatch for houses and outbuildings. The canons of Malton Priory took it for thatching from the Vale of Pickering and in the seventeenth century the manor court at Fylingdales prohibited the burning of 'Thatch Linge'.[1] From old pictures of Goathland and Beckhole we may surmise that formerly all the houses there were thatched with heather, just as Joseph Ford believed that they once all were in Great Fryup (*see plate* 4).[2] Ling was also used as a base with straw as the final covering. Both Spout House and Carr Cote, Bilsdale, have remains of ling in the thatch.

The use of heather most recently remembered is for the making of besoms. Although many farmers made their own, this, like the making of bee skeps, was a means of eking out a living by cottagers and smallholders. In the last century there lived on East Moors, north of Helmsley, an old couple, a mole-catcher and his wife, called Abbot. He made besoms and bee skeps, and kept bees for honey for sale, whilst his wife fashioned peggy sticks and pegs like gypsies' pegs. 'Ah've seen 'em many a time both smoking long clay pipes.' In the ashes on the hearth stood from one year's end to another a teapot to which a pinch of tea was added from time to time until the pot was full. Taking their goods for sale to Helmsley market, they used to buy a few ounces of black twist and six pairs of kippers, which twined together he carried home slung over his shoulder.[3]

Others remembered are Robert Hunton, Low Garth, Fryup, known as Besom House, and John Hall who, living at Pig Lug, Hartoft, a smallholding with two acres of grass and sixty acres of moor, brought up ten children. The house, now pulled down, derived its name from its appearance, with one chimney at one end like a pig's *lug* (ear). During the First World War John Hall took besoms to

[1] *The Honor and Forest of Pickering*, vol. IV, 1897, ed. R. B. Turton, NRRS; and NRRO, ZCG III 1/1.
[2] See also Alice Hollings, *Goathland*, 1971, p. 89.
[3] Mr I. Ventress, Wombleton.

Pickering by horse and trap to sell at 11*d.* a dozen, and a little later earned £5 12*s.* 6*d.* for fifty dozen.[1]

Sometimes the manufacture of scuttles was allied with besom-making, as may be seen in the photograph of George and Isaac Scarth of Glaisdale (*plate* 184). Scuttles were used for various carrying purposes and especially for picking and sorting potatoes. Made from plaited oak or ash bands with a length of hazel stick bent into an oval for the top, they are still being produced as a hobby by Mr Frank Gallon of Ugthorpe, whose father made them before him. 'I remember my Dad making one over the fire at night' (*see plate* 189). The Scarths took their wares round with a donkey and cart, and it is on record that one year they pulled ling from June to September 'and nivver a drop o' rain'.

Besom-making flourished as a minor industry at and near Pickering. Besides besoms supplied to farmers and sold at fairs, they were made by the thousand to send to the foundries of shipyards in the north of England and Scotland, mostly through dealers based at Pickering. Sold without handles, they were used for taking the scum off molten metal as it came out of the furnaces. If bits fell in they were burnt up; and after two sweeps the besom was done.

When this wholesale business began is not clear, but White's *Directory, North and East Ridings*, 1867, states that 'large quantities of besoms are made here, the moors furnishing abundant material', and seven makers in Pickering itself are listed. By 1890 there were still five in the town recorded in Bulmer's directory. One of them, William Appleby, fetched his ling from Saltersgate.

Within recollection besom-making was centred on the moorend farms at Stape, north of Pickering—farms wrested from the moor after the Enclosure Acts. Here the occupants of the scattered holdings, ranging from twelve to sixty acres, grew corn to feed to stock and earned a living chiefly by selling eggs, butter and besoms. It was said to us that 'You 'ed ter deu summat ter git *keeak* [cake]' and that your living depended on 'Self and guts and *yam* [home] at neets.'

Seventeen besom-makers—mostly Eddons, Allansons, Hollidays, Watsons and Wilfords—are recollected in the 1920s and 1930s on this side of Rawcliffe Bank (a hill on the Newton to Stape road). Many of their farms—High House, Stoney Moor, High Muffles, Grouse Cottage, High Leaf Howe for example—have been overtaken by afforestation or amalgamated with others, and various economic factors including the formation of the Milk Marketing Board in the 1930s as well as the decline in demand have spelled the virtual end of the trade.

Each farm had a besom house—usually a timber shed—containing nippers for holding the ling fixed to a work bench or wooden table, an 'esh 'oss' (ash

[1] Mr F. Hall, Pickering.

160. *Mr R. Smailes, Goathland, setting up turves to dry—two over one—on Goathland Moor.*

161. *Mr K. Eddon, Goathland, building rooks within sight of the Fylingdales Early Warning Station.*

TURF CUTTING

162. *Turf cutter's initial cut out to claim his swidden (1911).*

163. *Mr Percy Smith collecting a swarm of bees at Hutton-le-Hole* (c. 1926).

164. *About forty hives owned by Mr W. Clemmitt (Billy the Bee) of Appleton-le-Moors about to be taken to the moors in August 1950.*

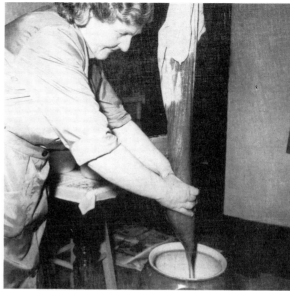

165. *Mr and Mrs H. Peirson, High Wind Hill, Hartoft, Rosedale, extracting honey in a straining cloth. The heated honey and comb is being poured in.*

166. *Mrs Peirson squeezes the honey out of the cloth. They do not use two sticks as in that method the honey runs down the arms.*

BEEKEEPERS

167. *Mr G. H. Leng, Sinnington, driving bees. He claps the bottom skep and the bees, disturbed, run up into the top skep, leaving behind combs filled with honey ready for extraction.*

168. *Mr T. Frankland, High Mill, Farndale, prepares briars for making bee skeps. First the thorns are stripped off with a piece of leather threaded with wire, then the briar is split, and lastly the pith scraped off.*

BEE SKEP MAKERS

169. *Mr T. Featherstone, Farndale, making bee skeps. Bundles of straw and split briars are at hand (1954).*

170. *Mr J. Skaife, Pickering, making a bee skep using cane instead of briars. The needle is slanted in and the cane threaded through the channel thus made. The wreath of straw is held tight by a segment of cow's horn.*

171. *The canes are joined by a knot.*

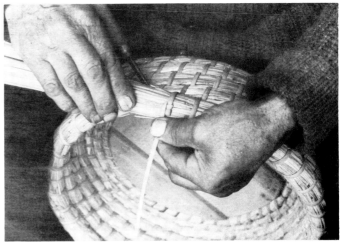

MOORLAND HARVEST

172. *Mr G. Featherstone and Miss R. Farrow of Hutton-le-Hole getting sieves at Venom's Nick, Rosedale.*

173. *Mr M. and Mr J. Graham, Hunt House, gathering brackens on Wheeldale Moor, Goathland.*

174–8. *Mr W. Holliday, Grange Farm, Stape, demonstrates cutting ling for besom making on Wheeldale Moor. Two pieces of ling are twisted together to make bands with which to tie up the sheaves. Note the ling sickle carried over his shoulder.*

179. *Mr Jack and Mr Jimmy Eddon, Stape Inn (Hare and Hounds), Stape, hammering the ash to separate the rings for making lappings (1911).*

180. *Raising the ash for lappings.* △

183. *Mr F. W. Holliday, Grange Farm, Stape, sets out for Pickering with a load of besoms (c. 1912).* ▷

◁ 181. *Jimmy Eddon splitting lappings.*

BESOM MAKERS

▷

184. *Mr Isaac and Mr George Scarth, makers of besoms, oak scuttles, and bee skips, Rock Head Cottage, Glaisdale. George is arranging a bundle of ling and Isaac is working the nippers with his foot and putting on lappings (c. 1885).*

◁

182. *Working the nippers to hold the ling tight and holding the pricker to make holes for the lappings.*

horse), a stand to hold the log of ash for raising bands for *lappings*, a pricker for piercing holes through the ling to insert the lapping, a chopper (often made from a length of an old lye) and a chopping block (*see plates* 179–82). Near the farm buildings stood a stone trough in which a piece of the trunk of an ash was steeped.

Farmers on the Keldy Castle estate were allowed to cut ling, and although living so close to the moors, they often had to travel five or six miles to find suitable long straight ling. It was best harvested when not full of sap. But except in wet weather or during the grouse nesting season ling was harvested throughout the year.

The besom-maker set off for the moor armed with a leather knee pad and a toothed ling sickle tucked over his shoulder. The former was necessary because he 'knelt on one knee bent for t' day', and the latter had the serrations on one side for a right-handed man and on the other for a *gallock*-handed. Holding the ling with one hand, he cut as low as possible with the other (*see plates* 174–8).

The ling was tied up in sheaves with ling bands, made by pulling up two pieces by the roots, laying the root ends together, then 'bind, twist, pull twist, then put between the legs and plait each end', lastly twisting round and round it was pulled tight. 'Ah kin mak 'em wi' mi eyes shut', said Mr Walter Holliday, who demonstrated cutting ling for us. Thirty sheaves, or a score and a half, were a day's work, and long stacks of sheaves of ling, piled up at the roadside to await transport, were formerly familiar sights on the moor.

Meanwhile ash bands had been prepared by choosing a small ash tree in a wood and trying it out for its suitability for raising lappings by cutting and braying a piece. Then a log about 3 feet 6 inches was sawn off, and if dry soaked in the ash trough. After the bark had been peeled off with a draw knife, it was hammered and hammered back and front up and down until a thickness of four or five rings of years growth two inches wide was raised. This was separated into strips of one year's growth, cut with a knife to one inch broad, nicked half way across the thickness and split again by hand so that the besom-maker had ready two lappings of half a year's growth. When they were put on, the shiny split side was turned outwards.

Often working as a team—perhaps a husband and wife—one gathered the bunches of ling together on the work bench, and the man worked the nippers with his foot. The pricker was inserted, a lapping pushed into the hole made, brought through and wound tightly round twice; then using the pricker again the end of the lapping was inserted under the tight band, bent back and tucked under a second time. Four or five lappings were usual on besoms for foundries, nine for stables and seven for general farm use. Lastly the nose was chopped off and a handle of hazel, knotted and peeled, was knocked in, if required. If all had been prepared beforehand, 'Ah've known,' says Tom Allanson, 'me and mi Dad mak twenty dozen besoms in a day.'

On Mondays a procession of men with their horses and flat carts, laden with bundles of besoms tied up in half dozens, set off for Pickering to deliver to agents and perhaps to barter half for provisions and sell half for cash (*see plate* 183). Agents such as the Hebdens might have 3,000 besoms stored for despatch, and they sometimes had orders for small ling whisks for brushing cloth in West Riding mills. Latterly the price paid for besoms increased to 2*s*. 6*d*. even to 5*s*. a dozen. They used to be sold at Egton Fair for 5*d*. each, about 1950 were retailed at 1*s*., and when made in 1970 were 7*s*. 6*d*. each.

On a farm there were always a clean besom outside the door for brushing dirty boots, and older besoms in stables and cowsheds. Like everything else on the moorlands every bit was used:

> '*We've had a good day, and we'll have a good neet,*
> *Put t' besom in t'fire and we'll have a good leet.*'

BEES

'THIS may be called a Bee-country;' wrote Marshall, '—especially the Morelands and the northern margin of the Vale; where great numbers of bees have usually been kept; and great quantities of honey collected; chiefly from the flowers of the heath; which afford an abundant supply.'

In the Middle Ages honey and beeswax from bees living in the trunks of trees in the Forest of Pickering belonged to every freeman, who had the honey found in his own woods.[1] It was then as important to the livelihoods of the inhabitants as it still was to many within recollection. At the present day, although beekeeping has declined in the last fifteen years, there are, excluding any towns, 455 bee-keepers with some 1,600 hives in the moorland dales and villages on the out-skirts in an area taken from Helmsley to East Ayton to Whitby to Guisborough. In the old days some depended on it for most or part of a living; others made a few shillings from bees as a *backwatch*. But by and large most now pursue it as a hobby.

Many of the people who keep bees have done so since childhood. Mr J. Skaife of Pickering says that his family have been beekeepers for 150 or more years, and that his father was one from birth when a hive was set aside for him. He had twelve acres and his bees—'they made the money'. Similarly Mr E. Calvert, shoemaker of Grosmont, now in his eighties, describes how one day when he was eight years old a hive of bees was going to swarm. His parents said 'if I came sharp home with the groceries I could have it'. On his return he found that his mother had taken the swarm and collected it in a straw skep for him.

True beekeepers are dedicated to their chosen task. 'It came natural to me,' says Mr W. Clemmit of Appleton-le-Moors who has kept bees since he was four-teen. About forty years ago he bought a special field in which to put his eighty hives. 'Ya ha' to have patience wi' bees. Ah used to sit watching 'em for hours. It's nice to know 'em; they're intelligent. Ah love 'em. They know if you're gentle.'

[1] *The Honor and Forest of Pickering*, vol. II, 1895, ed. R. B. Turton, NRRS.

John Skaife's father thought so much about his bees that he 'cared more for them than bairns'. A story goes that one night whilst undressing before going to bed he found a bee stuck in his waistcoat. He put it into an empty match box and placed it to warm by the dying embers of the fire. Then taking it out into the orchard he let it go into one of his ninety hives. If this had been the wrong one the bees would have killed an unladen bee. But they didn't. 'He knew it out of all the millions he had.'

Marshall wrote of a general mortality amongst bees in the winter of 1782–3, which he put down either rightly or wrongly to a lack of bee bread (pollen and honey with which the larvae are fed). Stocks were plainly built up again, but the devastation caused to the old black English bees by Isle of Wight disease during the First World War is still bemoaned by beekeepers.

The English bee was better tempered and more suited to the climate than imported ones. Some men search for wild bees in woods where they might have lived since before that time in an endeavour to build up the old strain again. Owing to choked cells wild bees are small but grow larger in hives. Although a few, such as Mr G. H. Leng of Sinnington, one of the experts of the district, have built up stocks with no yellow on them (part of the colour of the Italian bees), and others claim that they still have original stock unaffected by disease, it is assumed that except perhaps in a very few places a hybrid strain now acclimatized to local conditions prevails.[1]

Modern beekeeping comes close to a science and ancient bee lore is remembered only if it has a direct bearing on good practice. Such is the sage advice given by Harold Leng that 'you can learn a lot you want to know by watching the entrance to the hive'. Superstition is all but forgotten.[2] Robert Hunton, the besom-maker of Fryup, always told the bees of deaths in the family and hung a piece of black material over the front of the hive. Others took the bees a piece of death cake, 'same as you give the mourners, sponge cake or summat o' that'. When a swarm was in flight, 'gonging the bees' as it was called, was usual. Either a pewter plate was hit with a fork, or a bell tolled, or more generally because quickest to hand fire-irons were rattled, 'tollin' t'reckons' (reckons struck with a poker), so that the parish knew that the bees were swarming. The noise in fact announced that the swarm was being followed by the owner. Formerly they might fly five or six miles with the beekeeper chasing after them. Occasionally a church tower, such as Lastingham, was their objective.

The significant change in beekeeping practice, the gradual replacement of straw

[1] Mr J. R. Cowton, Official Inspector of Bees for the North Riding.
[2] See Rev. J. C. Atkinson, *Forty Years in a Moorland Parish* (1893), 1923 edition, pp. 126–8.

skeps by wooden hives beginning in the 1880s, is well remembered by the elderly.[1] Straw skeps used to be kept in bee boles (recesses in a south-facing wall), which are fairly rare in our area; in a beehouse, of which we have seen only one, at Dale Head, Westerdale (*see plate* 223); and in general on beestones, flat circular stones with a projecting lip (*see drawing on page* 92).

Straw skeps, taking almost a day to make and formerly sold at 4*s*. or 5*s*. apiece, used to be the chief outlay in beekeeping. Bees naturally build combs in a circle and preferred skeps, and were kept warmer in them in winter than in wooden hives. But they were damaged by rain and inconvenient to manage. The normal sized skep could be added to by putting a cap (small skep) on top or placing an imp (a large shallow straw ring) underneath. The cap was easily taken off and the comb of honey cut out. People used partially to block the entrance with a small flat piece of wood with holes on the bottom side to keep out mice.

Many people made bee skeps of either rye or wheat straw (*see plates* 169–71). They are still in demand for taking swarms, for driving bees, and as extras to bring into use as hives in a good season. The Skaifes used to grow the wheat 'Little Joss' for them for its long pliant straw. This is first stripped of its feather with the thumb nail. Next, starting by nailing a *wreath* (a bunch of straw sufficient for a row) to a round piece of wood with hollowed sides, the skep-maker employs a needle and small sections of cow's horn, graded in size for use as the skep grows larger to hold each wreath as it is bound to the next. The binding material is now cane, but it used to be long lengths of briar (bramble) gathered in summer, hung up and seasoned for winter work. The thorns were stripped off with a small piece of leather, threaded with wire, bent in two, then the briar was split, and finally laid on the knee, the pith scraped off first with the mitt and then with the penknife (*see plate* 168).

In the old days of straw skeps it was the custom to smother bees to collect the honey and to avoid becoming overstocked. Usually the lightest and heaviest skeps were dealt with in this way, and the medium ones with young queens kept for stock. The lightest were chosen because they would not be likely to survive the winter, and Harold Leng thinks that by culling the oldest and heaviest the Isle of Wight disease was kept in check. In these skeps the mite had had time to run its course, and by destroying the bees they also destroyed the mite. He adds that it was not long after the modern hive had come into general use and the smothering of bees had almost ceased that the disease swept the country.

The method employed for smothering was to dig a round hole about a foot

---

[1] An entry in the account book of the joiner, Martin Sleightholm of Goathland, reads: '1887 Wm. Smith Hunthouse. Oct 6 New Beehive 9s.'

deep in the ground and to stick in the bottom one or more little forked sticks holding squibs of brown paper soaked in sulphur. These when lit made a suffocating smoke and the skeps with a bag put over them were held in turn over the pit.

It is remembered by Mrs H. Peirson, who lived at Birch House, Hartoft, that fifty years ago these occasions were called bee-takings and were as important as clipping or pig-killing days. At the backend when the honey flow had finished the neighbouring beekeepers gathered at the farm on an agreed evening. After the smothering, everyone helped to extract honey by lamplight in the back kitchen where a fire had been lit.

Honey used to be extracted by cutting the comb out of the frames and heating it in a pan or cauldron; or the comb could be taken out warm straight from the hive. It was poured into a funnel-shaped straining cloth made of a square of rough linen hung from a ceiling hook (*see plates* 165–6). Then clamps, two sticks held together by a strap which was gradually tightened, were drawn steadily up and down by two people to squeeze out the honey.

Eventually smothering went out and driving came in. For this a few puffs from a smoker into which had been put and lighted a piece of fuzzball (a fungus, one of the *Lycoperdons*) slightly anaesthetized the bees. One skep was placed over another upside down containing bees and honey, held apart by iron staples (*see plate* 167). When the bottom skep was clapped the bees disturbed ran up into the top one, thus leaving the bottom one containing the honey free of bees. The queen could be taken out and put in a box. John Skaife told us that they used to get 4*d.* for driven bees that had made 3½ to 4 stones of honey.

Bees usually swarm between May and July and 'a prime swarm', says Harold Leng, is generally taken in May. In the cool villages of the North Riding the second and third weeks in June are likely periods for swarming, usually any time between eleven in the morning and three in the afternoon. The first swarm contains the old queen and thereafter the high 'peep, peep, peep' of the virgins (young queens) can be heard by the bee-keeper listening intently close to the hive. Nowadays restrained by various means, such as clipping the wings of the queen, they may only cross a little field.

If bees choose a hollow tree in which to swarm they will go up not down. They know that if down the rain will drip on to them. If the swarm hangs on a tree trunk Will Clemmit uses a goose's or a duck's wing to sweep them off into a skep. The use of 'wings' is described by Henry Best in his *Rural Economy in Yorkshire in 1641*, and the use of fuzzball is mentioned by the Elizabethan, John Gerard, in his *Herball*. After the swarm has been collected in a straw skep this is turned on to a board in front of a wooden hive and the bees troop in like a regiment of soldiers.

Beekeeping is naturally a chancy business, and the flourish of the different flowers is noted throughout the seasons. Some of the earliest flowers are those of the gooseberry. In 1970 a beautiful flourish of hawthorn, not always of use because of the low temperature in May, was enjoyed. Besides fruit blossom, sycamore, white clover and bean flowers (not all of which are present in the moorland dales), wild flowers such as the Rosebay Willow Herb are valuable. Bilsdale is noted for its bluebells which make beautiful white honey, and Douthwaitedale for its lime trees which make pale green. In July and August bramble and in October ivy flowers come on.

In the past bees were moved about more often than they are today. One of the Skaifes used regularly to take eighty hives to the Wolds for the white clover and the *brassock* (charlock) then prevalent in the corn. Farmers have paid for bees to be brought to fields of beans or to orchards for pollination purposes. 'Now they spray everything; there's nothing to travel about for.'

The great exception to this is the annual transportation of hundreds of hives not only by local beekeepers but by many from a distance to the heather moors in August, usually from the 12th at the latest to the end of September. Great numbers, usually in a small enclosure near the shelter of a wall away from habitation, may be seen annually for instance at Saltersgate, on Rudland Rigg, and on Goathland, Egton, Wheeldale and other moors.

A report in the *Malton Messenger* describes how in late September 1856 the Rev. W. Long of Lythe was riding over the moors and at Saltersgate, where there were no fewer than 300 hives in a small enclosure adjoining the moor, he and his horse were severely stung so that he had to spend the night at Thornton-le-Dale 'dreadfully swollen'. Whether the weather was thundery, wet or windy, all conditions disliked by bees, is not related. But when working the heather bees can be very vicious and their stings more painful than usual, either because they have been disturbed by being moved or because they realize that their winter stocks are at stake. On the other hand a man may be hiving swarms all the season and hardly ever be stung.

Transporting a good number of hives to the moors involved hard work. (When Mr A. Jefferson of Staithes was given his first bees, he took them in a skep in a sack on a bus!) In the days of horses it could take over four or five hours for the beekeeper to reach his destination. When he was seven or eight John Skaife well remembers helping his father to take 150 hives, all except twenty-two or three of straw, to Staindale and to Whinney Nab near Saltersgate with horses and rulleys. Two loads of a dozen hives went each night for most of a week.

To prepare the bees for transport they were put to sleep with puffs from the smouldering fuzzball. For a straw hive a piece of cheese cloth was held at either side of the bottom of the skep, dexterously covering up the base as the hive was turned up. A tie was then put round. This enabled the bees to breathe en route. On the moor special boards had been prepared on which the hives were inverted and the cloths slowly drawn out. 'This was what I first learnt to do among beekeeping', says John Skaife.

The flow of nectar from heather can be taken by the bees at a lower temperature than for that from other flowers. Foraging bees range up to three miles and seeing them whizzing across the moors it is easy to understand that their wings fray off and their average working life is only a fortnight to six weeks. If the weather is right and the nectar flow is good they can fill a hive in a week.

Good and bad years for heather are remembered: '1887 was the best year ever' but another year (not specified) 'mi Dad went on to t'moors and there was nivver a flower of heather that would have made a button-hole'; 1933–5 and 1945 were excellent years. John Skaife recalls that in 1935 a 'straw stock' of theirs swarmed on 3rd August. They took it to the moor on 12th August with about half a pound of honey in it, and when they brought it back, they bottled 56 lb. from it. Twelve stones of honey from five hives is reckoned as very good. Heather honey, seldom pure as the bees go to other flowers near the moor, is too strong for some tastes (including William Marshall's) and is blended with other types. In good years beekeepers speak in terms of tons of honey.

Nowadays extractors and presses have mostly replaced the straining cloth method. Following extraction the remaining comb is purified to make beeswax. It is placed in a bag sometimes weighed down by a brick and heated in very hot but not boiling water in a copper. Tipped into a bucket the sediment drops to the bottom—a process repeated until the wax is clear. We have been shown deep yellow blocks of beeswax by the beekeepers, but John Skaife remembers that his father was once asked to take a swarm at a house where the bees might have been over fifty years and that the wax was as white as snow.

Some was kept for mixing with turpentine for making furniture polish. But again the sale of beeswax helped out the family budget. Tailors requiring it for waxing threads were customers. Years ago it was sold for 2s. 6d. a pound but latterly it usually was exchanged for equipment from the makers of bee appliances at 6s. 6d. a pound.

Honey used to be sold in buckets which held two to two-and-a-half stones, bought new every year. It was sometimes sold to factors such as the Simpsons, the bacon curers of Gillamoor, who bottled and sent it amongst other places to Harrods. It used to be retailed at 1*s.* in tall jars, and many people sold honey at the door to visitors.

Mead, called botchet, was one of the products of beekeeping. In former days yeast, latterly used as a fermenting agent, was unnecessary. The old beekeepers made mead from the residue from the bag left after squeezing for extraction, and as the whole contents of the skep had been cleared out, this contained enough pollen or some property from the straw of the skep to cause a good fermentation. Four to four-and-a-half pounds of the honey and wax to a gallon of water made a sweet mead and two pounds to a gallon a dry one. Botchet, which could be a potent drink, was taken into the harvest field and was also offered to wedding guests and the Christmas singers.

FRUIT

IN the villages and hamlets north and south of the moorlands, but especially in those of lower Ryedale and along the northern edge of the Vale of Pickering, gnarled fruit trees grow in old orchards and in the long narrow crofts which abut on to back lanes behind the houses in many villages. In those such as Harome, Wombleton, Nawton and Beadlam, orchards with neat rows of trees are shown on the map of the 1856 Ordnance Survey. Belonging to cottages, houses, small-holdings and farms, they formed part of the economy of this naturally fruitful countryside. Cottagers for instance partly relied on fruit to pay their rents.

Within recollection fruit growing and picking was a well-organized trade run by a few fruiterers and hucksters who themselves owned large orchards.[1] The season, lasting from the beginning of July until nearly Christmas, started with gooseberries, followed by red currants, black currants, and a few raspberries; it continued with plums throughout September and finally ended with pears and apples. In the winter the gardens and orchards required attention and the fruiterer often carried on the huckster's business of dealing in pigs, geese, rabbits, butter and eggs.

The fruit, invariably despatched from the railway station nearest to where it had been picked, usually Nawton, Sinnington and Kirkbymoorside, was disposed of in various ways. The bulk went in truck loads by rail to jam factories: Hartley's at Aintree, Tickler's at Grimsby, J. Smith of Shipley and many others including Holgate's and Moorhouse's of Leeds. The best quality was sent to shops in Whitby and Scarborough, and much went via wholesalers or on a commission basis to Leeds, Hull and Hartlepool, whilst what was over was sold in local markets.

During the season the fruiterer's men with horses and rulleys daily toured the

[1] Recollections of Mr J. Leaman, who worked for the Sunleys who had a four-acre garden at Nawton; Mr W. H. Swales, whose business goes back to 1872 to his grandfather, William Bowes; Miss L. Wilson, who with her sisters picked 'berries' (gooseberries); and Mr I. Ventress, who still grows fruit for sale to wholesalers: all are over eighty and all of Wombleton. Also of Mr J. W. Underwood of Kirkbymoorside, who worked for Mr S. H. Richardson who had an eight-acre nursery garden at that town.

◁ FRUIT

185. *The berry pullers (gooseberry pickers) taken at Tinley Garth, Kirkbymoorside, although they came from Wombleton (c. 1902). Front Row: Mr W. Bowes, Mrs J. Wilson, Mrs E. Best, Mrs M. Smith, Mr T. Richardson. Back Row: Alice Hill, Lily Craven, Annie Best, Agnes Smith, Lily Wilson, Minnie Smith, and Nanny the horse.*

186. *Vegetables and fruit for sale at Whitby Market. A man in a smock centre back sells cheese and fat bacon (?). Icecream, then licked from thick glasses, is being sold at the two stalls (1884).*

△ CORN DOLLIES

187. *Mr and Mrs S. Beeforth, Westerdale, with some of the corn dollies they have made.*

market towns and villages, especially Marton and Normanby, where they were 'squashed out with fruit' particularly gooseberries. Suitable containers—hampers for plums, barrels for apples and sacks for gooseberries—were left for families to fill. Snainton produced a great many red currants, whilst Thornton-le-Dale was famous for its raspberries, mostly grown for Holgate's who sent barrels for them.

When families were unable to gather the fruit themselves, the fruiterers organized 'flocks' of women and girls for the gooseberries and plums (*see plate* 185). The Wilsons as children picked before going to school and on their return in the evenings. When they grew up, wearing gloves and thick long-sleeved blouses they picked all day. In the early years of the century 1½*d*., later 2*d*. and 4*d*., was the rate per stone which took about an hour to pick. When the bushes, usually the varieties Leveller and Whitesmith with some Whinham's Industry, were young, it was possible for one woman to slip twenty to thirty stones of gooseberries in a day, but fifteen was more usual especially with older bushes.

John Leaman remembers that one year he dealt with 2,500 stones of gooseberries. Throughout the season he sent off from Kirkbymoorside station each Wednesday (market day) three trucks each containing two tons. William Swales says that in 1908 they sold eighty-seven and a half tons. When there was a glut the lowest price for gooseberries was £3 10*s*. a ton, and at such a time the fruit was pulped down at the factory and used for jam making in the winter.

In August to earn a little money, for instance to go on the annual Sunday School treat, mothers and children went into the country to gather wild crab apples. They shook the trees so that the fruit fell down and all that was required was to pick it up and fill sacks. The crab apples went to jam factories.

When it came to plums, this fruit posed a problem because it ripened quickly. Victorias were the favourites, followed by Early Prolific. Czars were difficult to sell. Every day they were sent by rail by the Richardsons at the rate of eighteen to twenty tons a week. In 1909 the Swales sold forty tons.

Both plums and apples were sent by rail in round hampers to Whitby market (*see plate* 186). Put on the train on Friday nights they arrived at Whitby at 7 a.m. next day. Meanwhile the fruiterer had travelled by train, then had gone round the shops taking orders, and later he or his employee 'stood' the market with any fruit left over. People from the dales flocked to buy it.

Cooking apples were mostly Bramley's Seedling, followed by Lane's Prince Albert, which suffered from canker. Lime bought by the truck load was used for whitewashing tree trunks or spread on the ground in the orchards. Besides selling apples at markets, the fruiterers sent the best to shops in Scarborough and sold whole barrels of them to individual farmers. Old Cockpit, a variety so called because it was later improved, went to Rowntrees at York for the 'boil houses' where jelly squares were made.

Amongst dessert apples every orchard had its Green Balsams, which still exist, and the almost equally popular Winer Pippins. Pears grown were usually Hazels, sold for eating. John Leaman remembers that in the spring he also despatched large quantities of eggs to Holgates for the making of lemon curd.

Although some fruit is still sold to wholesalers, fruit growing for sale on the scale described ended with the Second World War. During the war the trees deteriorated, cheaper foreign fruit pulp is now imported, and the springing up of local factories paying good wages has changed the pattern of life.

188. *Mr F. Bentley, Rudland Farm, near Gilla-moor, with a few of the sticks he has made. The small one is of blackthorn.*

189. *Mr F. Gallon, Ugthorpe, making scuttles from ash.*

WOODLAND CRAFTS

190. *Sawing and shaping clog soles in Arncliffe Woods, Glaisdale (1913).*

192. *Mr Nesswell Pennock, blacksmith (1861–1947), Linns Farm, Beckhole, Goathland, rimming a wheel. He was paid 3s. for each wheel. Although never apprenticed, Ness Pennock could make anything (c. 1920).*

OLD-TIME CRAFTSMEN

193. *Mr George Jackson, blacksmith at Hawsker near Whitby, and an apprentice (1875).*

191. *Mr Thomas Parker (1812–1902) thatcher, poet and local antiquarian, who lived at Wombleton.*

194. *Mr Jack Lumsdan, beginning at the eaves and going upwards, stobs straw in with a swallow tail at Hollins Farm, Farndale (1938).*

195. *Using the shaver for trimming a 'breead'.*

THATCHING

196. *The* **back** *of the house with thatch continuing on to an outshut. A large turf stack adjoins the house on the right.*

197. *The finished thatch.*

198. *Mr Seth Eccles, thatcher, of Helmsley holding a bundle of straw at Oak Hill, Farndale. He does not use the old stobbing method of thatching.*

199. *Sharpening spits for thatching with a whittling hook at Oak Hill, Farndale.*

HOUSES

200. *Raking down the thatch before trimming with sheep shears.*

201. *Cutting off the bottom of the thatch with an easing knife.*

STONE MASONS

THE dominant factor about work in stone in the moorland valleys, especially Eskdale, is the quality and excellence of the stone available for building. From the beds of the Jurassic rocks worked in innumerable quarries in all the dales, stone was raised for abbeys and churches, for mansions built from the eighteenth to the early twentieth century, for railway bridges, for large civil engineering projects, for buildings in the towns of Teesside, for houses in the villages and farmhouses on the hillsides.

The different beds yielded stone with particular characteristics of which the most typical was the sandstone, or freestone as it is called, worked in quarries throughout the Esk valley and its tributary dales. Thousands of tons of freestone were shipped to London by the Whitby Stone Company formed in 1834 at the time of the making of the Whitby to Pickering Railway,[1] and the name 'Postgate', found here more than once, means quarry road from post, the face of the quarry, and the Old Norse *gata*, a road.

When hewn green, the freestone used for building is easily worked and hardens on exposure to the air. It is always laid in horizontal strata and is in *threads* (beds) conveniently separated by thin layers of sand, silt or clay. In general yellow in colour darkening to brown and sometimes stained blue at the top by heather, it is raised in massive seams (blocks). When these blocks are cut up, the wallstones conveniently come out at 9 inches or 10 inches high. This factor, common to other local quarries, as well as the ease in dressing, determined the method of building; that of large stones of ashlar masonry laid in even courses, so evident in Eskdale and its tributary dales.

'Good building stone', say the masons, 'is workable, dependable, and all of a colour.' 'Stone should be malleable and velvety, not coarse like sugar.' 'Stone is a living thing, not a piece of dead matter.'

Some of the masons in the valleys of the north-east moorlands have been and are outstanding. John Castillo (1792–1845), the son of an Irishman living most of

[1] C. Fox-Strangways, *The Jurassic Rocks of Britain*, vol. I, Yorkshire, 1892; and T. H. English, *Whitby Prints*, vol. II, 1931.

his life in the Lealholm district, was also a poet.[1] A good example of his and his colleagues' skill are the buildings of Stonebeck Gate Farm, Little Fryup (*see plan on page* 3). Here none of the many doorways has wooden surrounds. Instead the stone jambs are rebated to allow the doors to fit flush. A curiosity is a set of stone steps, carved from a single block of freestone, now at Danby museum, but formerly making a stairway to a loft in the buildings of Lumley House, Danbydale.

In Farndale John Foord built Hollins and Frost Hall (originally called Frost Hole) in the 1820s, both showing fine work—including segments (shallow arches), ashlar facing stones and massive stones for the lower courses. A later member of the family, Joseph Ford (1870–1944) who was born at Hamer House, left school when he was twelve, and as a farm lad planned to emigrate to Canada. By chance helping to build Cropton chapel, he found his métier and eventually settled as a mason at Castleton. We have quoted from his book, *Some Reminiscences and Folk Lore of Danby Parish and District*.

Amongst other masons were George Harland (1882–1969) of Glaisdale who left notes published in 1970 as a booklet under the title *Queen of the Dales*, and Mr Fred Handley, who started work when he was eleven and remembers walking from Farndale to Castleton with his father, mason on the Feversham estate, to build the Moorlands Hotel. Moving to Helmsley after the First World War, he pioneered large-scale private housing developments there.

Another family of masons, to whom we are indebted for much of the information in the rest of this chapter, go back to William Weatherill (1777–1866) who in 1810 settled as a mason and quarryman at Spout House, a seventeenth-century house next to the old Sun Inn in Bilsdale. The two acres, which went with it and on which they kept a cow and a few hens, 'was hardly enough' say their descendants. William's son, another William (1815–1892), had seven children, of whom the four sons—John, William, Thomas and Davison—all followed the same trade of mason and quarryman. Masons quarried in winter. 'They were usually all right up to Christmas, then it was a hit and miss job.' Jack, son of Davison, for many years the mason at Rievaulx Abbey, amassed a fund of knowledge of medieval work and the tools employed.

The fortunes of one branch of the family may be taken as an example of a craftsman's life in the last century and in this. Thomas (1850–1931) was apprenticed to an uncle, a blacksmith at Castleton, but he 'swallowed t'anvil'—that is, he left, and putting his budget on his back, he walked back to Spout. From here he worked quarries in Raisdale whence stone was sent via Sexhow station by rail to

[1] D. Quinlan, *John Castillo, Bard of the Dales*, 1968; and G. M. Tweddell, *Bards and Authors of Cleveland and South Durham*, 1872.

Hartlepool and Stockton. In between he turned to other jobs. Masons were numerous, and often had to seek work miles from home. Many lodged from Monday to Saturday, paying 3s. 6d. a week and taking their own food in a big basket. At weekends they cycled or walked home.

In 1904 Thomas, then on the move and hearing that stone was required for the building of Crathorne Hall near Yarm, took Shaw End Quarry, near Lealholm; at the same time a smallholding of eighteen acres close to it became vacant and he moved there with his family including four sons, Thomas, Jack, Frank and Bill, all either already or about to become masons. Bill lost an arm in the First World War which ended his career with stone; and the rest adopted their own masons' marks as had Castillo and earlier men before them.

The area of Shaw End included a complex of freestone quarries that in the last century had been extensively worked for stone for shipment from Whitby to London. From the escarpment where it is situated on the south side of Eskdale back to back with Postgate Quarry in Glaisdale, you look down on the little farmstead on a terrace of hill and across Great Fryup. 'Milking', say the Weatherills, 'started your days and got you warm.' Members of the family were musical, several of them playing the fiddle. When he was a boy Bill had to be able to play two hymn tunes, 'Belmont' and 'When Mothers of Salem', before he could go to the annual treat, Stokesley Show.

In the quarry they had a stone-built blacksmith's shop, a knocking up shop, a loading crane, and gear brought from Raisdale. 'It was like a second home.' Frank, who had made a grindstone for sale before he left school, started work young. He blew the bellows of the forge for his father; for in line with the versatility of the old-time craftsmen, Thomas, trained as a blacksmith, forged his own tools, sharpened and steeled picks, made rollers, wedges, and mended chains. Frank himself was eventually able to say that he had done all but face a hammer. He too, like former masons, has pursued antiquarian interests.

The quarry belonged to Lord Downe, to whom 6d. a ton royalty was paid. Trade at first was good, and then spasmodic. Supplying stone for Crathorne Hall was their first order and some blocks for the portico were 10 feet long and weighed 3 tons. At that date the price was 1s. 0½d. per cubic foot, with the addition of 2d. for stones over 6 feet long and more for exceptionally large ones. They were carted to Lealholm station by horses and a stone waggon.

At the hall Thomas, the eldest brother, was working with 100 other banker-hands dressing stones. A banker was the bench on which stone was dressed with the chisel, and the head banker mason in charge of the measurements was the shop *coddy*. They wore 'pinnies', whilst quarrymen wore sheepskin jackets to keep out the wet. George Harland's father, a head freestone quarryman, a much respected position, wore a box hat. 'Mansions and churches,' says Frank, 'were the pastures of the stone masons once on a time.'

Just before and after the turn of the century a number of churches in the district were either built or restored, many of them by the architect Temple Moore and the builder R. P. Brotton of Chop Gate, Bilsdale, who employed one or other members of the Weatherill family on some of them. When in 1903 Danby church was very extensively restored in memory of Canon Atkinson, Thomas and his son, Jack, quarried the stone for it at Ainthorpe Rigg Quarry and were paid at the rate of 1½d. per hour. Jack (1889–1960) worked at the re-building of Lythe church near Whitby in 1910. Stone was raised from the cliff just below, and hoisted up by hand crane in quarter of a ton and ton blocks; and the mortar was mixed with a flail with an iron swipple. Thomas had dressed much of the face-work for Kildale Hall in 1899, whilst Jack and Frank together with others built a new wing and garden walls at Egton Lodge about 1911.

It is recorded that in the first year at the quarry J. and T. Light, local masons and great cricketers working in old Shaw End quarry near by, made by hand with tools borrowed from the Weatherills the Lealholm cricket roller, and that wrapped round with old ropes, it was dragged to the cricket field by the Lights with two youths grasping the handle and a long line of village children holding a strong rope either pulling or when going downhill holding it back.

Over the years the Weatherills supplied stone for schools, churches and war memorials, built garages, supplied chimney pots, grindstones, dairy shelves—all the usual masons' jobs. In 1933 the last big undertaking was Bramble Carr, Ainthorpe, altered and enlarged for a Harley Street specialist, and for which old stone was partly used. Putting all his skill into it, Jack Weatherill regarded this as his major work. It is worth recording that the three sons of George, son of Jack, are the sixth generation of the family to be stone masons.

Shaw End Quarry ceased to be worked by the family in 1959, but it is still used occasionally by a local builder. Of the eleven quarries drawn on when Crathorne Hall was being built, it is the only one kept open. The towering posts of fine yellow rock fifty feet high are still impressive. 'A stone man', says George Weatherill, 'would be excited. His living's there.'

A common means of obtaining freestone was from tumblers, that is, boulders that might weigh up to 300 tons, which had literally tumbled down the hillside from an escarpment. They were not loose outcrop, but often fine quality stone. 'A good tumbler and you're made' (*see plates* 205, 206, 207).

The aim in cutting one up was to get out the largest pieces first, turning the tumbler over with crow bars and cutting again and again. Bearing in mind the colour and the quality, the mason made use of all he could; as George Harland said, 'Same as a piece of cloth for a dress.'

In 1869 Thomas Weatherill senior, then in his teens, and his father had supplied the cover stone, measuring about 7 feet square and weighing approximately 7 tons, and cut from a tumbler near Spout House, for the monument to the second Baron Feversham by Sir Giles Gilbert Scott in Helmsley market-place. Having only one bar and a cart shaft with which to move it they squared and quarried it with great difficulty.

Before the mid eighteenth century masons built either in rubble walling or in courses with rough-dressed squared oblong wallstones; but from that time onwards, using to advantage the nature of the local stone, they developed methods of dressing the face of stonework familiar to anyone with an observant eye on the buildings in the valleys. This more sophisticated work coincided with a spate of general building and rebuilding. The forms of finish are herringboning, scutching, slew axing, diamond hammering, batting, draughting used for margins, and the Victorian rock-faced (natural and deep rock) employed for instance on railway bridges (*see plates* 208–11).

Herringbone, the earliest finish, and scutching, popular in the nineteenth to the early twentieth century, are especially characteristic. The former, inspired by the shape of the backbone and bones of a herring or kipper, developed two forms, a plain ribless (the rib being the backbone) generally used on farm buildings and simple dwellings, and the draughted finely axed, showing a neat rib, running horizontally across the centre of the wallstone, and employed on mansions and yeomen's dwellings (*see plate* 211).

The oldest mason always dressed the stones for the farmhouse and the rest worked on the buildings. An axe, a curved pick shaped like an anchor with a flat shaft 2 feet long, is used on the stone placed on end (*see plate* 209). Having ruled a line with a piece of black slate (which does not stain) across the middle, the mason first draughts round the outside, and begins herringboning at one end driving the axe from the outer edge to the centre. He then turns the stone round and dresses the other end.

For scutching the mason stands the stone on end and, using a scutching hammer, into either end of which may be fitted different widths of bits (the most usual $\frac{5}{8}$ inch), he strikes on the back edge of the point to make shallow oblong marks. Again there are two types, one spaced in rows, and the other alternating neatly to form a basketwork pattern. A skilled scutcher could dress a stone almost like chiselling and much more quickly, so that this facing was sometimes used to dress all sides of the stone. Masons of necessity sharpened the bits themselves. The bankerhands often said that the chap who invented the scutching hammer should have had to use them all himself, as it was horsework. A quarryman's sample, a small square weight-shaped stone, with a ring at the top to hold it by, had three sides faced with herringboning, scutching, chiselling, and the fourth was clean dressed that is, smooth and flat.

It was reckoned that a full kit for a skilled mason was about 300 pieces of all the various tools and instruments necessary to carry out a first-class job. To mention a few, there were mallet-headed chisels ranging from the point on to $\frac{1}{4}$ inch up to 4 inches. The inch was the general draught size; above that they were called boasters, and the 3 inches and 4 inches, batting tools. There were pitch and corking tools, the latter for grooving for leaded windows and general relief work, a 4 to 6 lb. mash hammer for punch and pitch work, a *kevel*, a walling hammer for rough dressing, the axes and scutching hammers already mentioned, Lewises and clips for lifting large blocks and many others (*see plate* 207).

The Weatherills mainly used tools from Manchester Mills and Brayshaws of Sheffield. When a group of six or ten masons were working on a job and the tools came back from sharpening at the blacksmith's, the shout went out 'Mill up'. The men stood in a circle in the shed, and the foreman picked up the tools and handed them round. Each man claimed his own and passed on the others.

Wallstones were usually dressed on the job, hence the sheds for the banker-hands. They measured 18 inches to 2 feet long by 6 or 7 inches wide on the bed and 7 inches to 1 foot high. Formerly when the fixers were building walls, they bedded the stones in mud, cow dung and grass, and up to about the 1930s there were no cavity walls. The blocks used for a chimney were called collars, because to avoid joints the centre of a cube of stone was chiselled out, and, so it was said, the masons carried these up round their necks. Eighteenth-century chimneys were in fact composed of only three stones, two large ones, 30 inches square, fitting one on top of the other like boxes without lids or bottoms, and the narrow capping, the top stone, projecting all round 3 inches.

Stone drinking troughs, a feature of the whole district, are seen by the roadside and on every farm both near the buildings and in the fields. Supplied by masons, they were priced according to how many gallons of water they held. The small ones, more difficult to make, hardly paid, and swine troughs were round with a hump in the middle on to which the food was poured.

Isaac Ventress tells us that his grandfather, George Ventress, of East Moors, a mason, made two for Highfield House, Nunnington in lower Ryedale. One, worth three gold sovereigns, made to serve three foldyards, was 10 feet 8 inches long, 3 feet 3 inches wide and 2 feet 6 inches high, outside measurements. Transported the ten miles on a heavy sledge over the snow one frosty morning, it was manœuvred into position on rollers.

The Weatherills charged at the rate of 1*s.* a gallon for making troughs up to the First World War. The size was based on whether they were required for pigs, cattle, horses, boiling potatoes, occasionally for pickling hams and so on. Because a horse paws, troughs for them had to be heavy, and for cattle they had to be 'liners'; that is, several in a row with the water flowing on gargoyles from one to another, because cattle foul water with their saliva and like it clean.

Walls for sheep breaks (T- and L-shaped), in gardens, and as fences round fields in all the upper parts of the dales (with hedges lower down) are usual. Years ago, Jack Weatherill has recorded, walling was mostly a winter pastime—'a few shillings a week and a bit o' dinner affair, when there was nowt else ti git'. The rate was 10*d.* to 1*s.* a rood (7 yards), a good day's work, so that six days a week at the lesser rate meant 5*s.*, that is £13 a year. If the rent was £2 it left £11 to bring up the children, not forgetting the little bit put by for a rainy day. 'This was about what my Grandfather would get at the early end of his time.'

The stones for walls are often squared quarry material; the *thruffs* or binders, 18 inches wide, do not project, and are placed one every square yard not in courses. The waller had to mark them, or 'he was lost'. The height is four feet with a coping which may be plain flat, square set, Scotch or Billycock hat (Gothic). The very different character of the walls, and of the houses, from those seen in the western dales of Yorkshire is an object lesson in the influence of local material on the appearance of the landscape.

202. Horses drinking at a trough; behind it a pump (now gone) at Park Gates, Pickering (c. 1929).

STONEWORK

203. Bee House at Dale Head, Westerdale. Now partially ruined, it is dated 1832. The arches and supporting columns are beautifully draughted. Note the two straw skeps with caps.

204. Mr John (Paddy) Peirson, postman of Goathland, drinks at the stone trough near New Wath (c. 1932).

205. *Mr Robert Weatherill (son of Frank) and his son Michael, cutting up a tumbler brought down by a landslip near Roger House, Danbydale, about 1920. He is making holes with a pick for the wedges.*

206. *'Teeathing', that is, putting in wedges to cut the stone across the grain. 'Boarding' is to place the wedges with the grain.*

207. *Using a crane and clips to move a block of stone.*

208. *Mr F. Weatherill, Ainthorpe, using a scutching hammer.*

209. *Mr F. Weatherill, Ainthorpe, dressing a stone with herringboning.*

210. *Doorway at Postgate Farm, Glaisdale, showing a good bold batting finish and the draughting round the borders. Lines would be drawn with black slate and then cut with a point and mallet.*

211. *Mr G. Weatherill points out herringbone work with the rib showing on the porch of the Roman Catholic church, Lealholm.*

212. *Mr T. E. Whittaker, Littlebeck, carver and ecclesiastical furniture maker, making a sanctuary chair.*

CABINET MAKERS

213. *Mr T., Mr E. W. and Mr T. W. Varley, Whitby, making a mahogany bookcase (1949).*

JOINERS AND WHEELWRIGHTS

AS we have shown in house building and implement making the resources of the country played an important part in the work of craftsmen, particularly of those working in wood. The oaks and of less importance the ashes, also elms, hollies, alders, hazels and hawthorns of the Forest of Pickering, had been felled for one purpose or another over the centuries. Even by the fourteenth century the forest with its great oaks, its saplings, themselves fifty years old, and *dotterels* (oaks with broken tops) had been greatly diminished—its trees used for the building and repair of abbeys and castles, for houses both great and small, for the building of ships, for the smelting of iron, for making ploughs, wains, carts, barrels, dishes, bowls, for fuel, and even for burning for kippering herrings.

The medieval method of 'respringing' continued in William Marshall's day and is described by him as cutting down trees a few inches above ground, leaving as much bark as possible and letting the young shoots grow. It was also customary to encourage *standells*, shoots left in cutting a hedge, to grow into trees, thus providing wood for small tools. In the eighteenth and nineteenth centuries many private woodlands were planted, and in the twentieth the tens of thousands of acres taken over by the Forestry Commission have brought back dense woodland to the region but in the form of soft wood—larch, spruce and pine.

The ability of the farmer and farm man to turn his hand to the making and repairing of any tool or simple implement no doubt stems from long tradition. This self-sufficiency was complemented by the work of the joiner, of whom there were one or more in every village or dale. Several lived on small farms; some moved from them to establish fairly large businesses, such as the Harrisons who started at Stuntry Carr, a smallholding between Goathland and Egton Bridge, and moved to Grosmont. Apprenticed one to another and using hand tools requiring a maximum of labour, they passed on old skills from generation to generation.

In many joiners' shops are still to be seen large and small lathes, wheel stools, wands and adzes for making wheels, patterns for plough beams and handles lying on rafters or stored in lofts, rows of augers once kept as bright as silver with constant use, and filled in or covered up saw-pits. From conversations with joiners and the entries in account books belonging to their fore-elders ranging from the 1840s to the early 1900s a picture emerges of life and work in the villages.[1]

All speak of going into the woods for timber. The Dawsons went in winter to Mulgrave Woods where they chose and marked hard-wood trees. The Sleight-holms obtained theirs from Littlebeck and the Harrisons had woods of their own. 'You were always watching for wood for certain jobs.' 'A country wheelwright was a past master at cutting wood to advantage, and he could tell at a glance how each tree could best be utilized.' Elms, with boles of the right dimensions, pre-ferably rock grown and gnarled, were selected for *nafs* (hubs). Timber was stored on the north side of a building for a year, cross cut into suitable lengths for different jobs, then sawn up in the saw-pit and laid on drying shelves for five years.

At each side of the saw-pit were stringers, long pieces of wood, and transomes, heavy pieces, laid across to support the tree. A plumbline let down into the pit helped to guide the bottom sawyer, who during a day 'lifted many a ton'. Not only planks but shaped sections such as plough beams were sawn out with the whip-saw. Sometimes to save transport trees were sawn up on a saw-horse rigged up on a hillside on the spot.

Rates of pay in the 1840s ranged from 2s. to 2s. 6d. or 3s. a day, and did not increase throughout the century. Hours were long, often from 6.30 in a morning to 6.30 at night, and jobs frequently entailed walking many miles there and back in the day carrying tools including a whip-saw for use on the farmer's saw-horse.

The versatility of the craftsmen, the small sums paid for his products and the constant repair work are noticeable in the ledgers. He was able to re-cog mill wheels, to make wands for windmills, to supply simple domestic furniture—in 1894 a 'New dresser and rack complete' for £2 15s. He made coffins for from £2 to £3 2s. 6d., ploughs in the 1840s and 1870s for 15s. 6d., waggons, carts, mangers, sheep troughs, pig creels, signboards, bee feeders, 'a cowcumber frame', a 'New box for stuft birds' and much besides. Competition was keen, bargains were struck, and sometimes for a large amount people paid small sums on account.

Apprentices spent day after day from six in the morning until six at night

---

[1] Mr G. C. Watson, Sneaton, Mr G. and Mr J. Harrison, Grosmont, Mr B. Knaggs, Hawsker. Account books lent by Mr F. Dawson, Newholm, Mr W. Tinsley, Farndale, Mr J. Sleightholm. Goathland and Miss V. Tomlinson, Appleton-le-Moors.

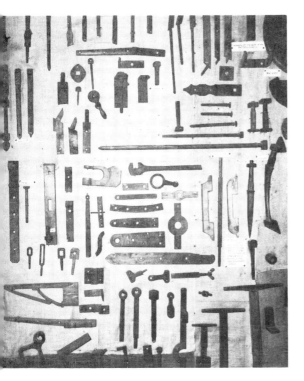

214. *Wooden patterns made by Mr George Tomlinson (1810–94) of Appleton-le-Moors for the iron parts of a waggon* (R.F.M.).

215. *Mr J. H. Tomlinson, great-grandson of George Tomlinson, joiner of Appleton-le-Moors, with the cant used for transporting wood for the building of Christ Church, Appleton in 1863–5* (R.F.M.).

JOINERS AND WHEELWRIGHTS

216. *Mr G. Harrison, Grosmont, joiner and wheelwright, now retired, with a desk he is making.*

217. *Mr J. Sleighthoom, Goathland, demonstrates boring a hole in the naf of a wheel for a bush.*

218. *Workshop of the Bensons, millwrights and ageicultural engineers, Ruswarp. Plough beams, reared up against the building, are seasoning. Mr J. H. Benson is the centre figure; on the right is Mr T. Crosby, who worked for them for fifty years, and on his left Mr T. Pegg (c. 1900).*

PLOUGH MAKERS

219. *Mr G. C. Watson and his father, Mr T. Watson, who is holding the front axle of a waggon. The North Cave plough was the last they made. To make one from start to finish took two days (1951).*

sawing in the saw-pit, and were given the job of making rakes (once with twenty-two teeth, then with eighteen, now with fourteen). So much time was allowed to do a given job. For instance Fred Dawson, apprenticed to his father for 23s. a week, out of which 10s. went for his keep, was allowed two and a half hours to make and white lead a square butter tub. 'Then after twenty years the housewife would complain if it leaked.' John Tinsley's advice to his son was 'Take time, learn to do it well, then do it quicker.' Mr W. W. Featherstone of Lastingham often made rolling pins from sycamore to give as wedding presents.

Entries for supplying coffins and making arrangements for funerals occur from time to time. In 1887 Martin Sleightholm made a child's coffin for 1s. 9d. Fir, pine, redwood and oak were used. The Tinsleys often put the age of the person alongside the entry. A funeral arranged in 1899 at Appleton-le-Moors by the Tomlinsons provided for a very good oak coffin with brass furniture, eight chosen bearers 1s. each, the use of hearse, cab and carriages, two bottles of British wine at 1s. each, cheese, and funeral cakes and bread cooked free of charge by Mrs Tomlinson: in all costing £6 12s. 6d.

Both the Dawsons and the Sleightholms describe the labour of making a coffin. To shape a side, the former wedged a board in a wall, put water and sand on it, lit a smouldering fire of shavings and chips below it, and steamed and bent it into shape; whilst the latter cut eight half circles at the shoulder of the side down to $\frac{1}{8}$ of an inch, then poured on boiling water to bend it. The sides were then quickly nailed down to the coffin board held down by a 4-lb. weight. The inside of ordinary coffins was coated half way up with pitch often heated in a pan on the kitchen fire. When oak was used it was an inch thick, so the coffin itself might weigh $12\frac{1}{2}$ stones.

Martin Sleightholm, grandfather of the present retired joiner, Jim Sleightholm, came from a farm at Hawthorn Hill, Goathland, to a then old workshop in that village in 1885, some of the first entries in his ledger read:

March 21	Misses Agre Lease rig New Latther [ladder] 18 rounds	8s.
March 25	Colection box for Esk Valley Chapel made stright fer wood	2s.
May 26	Methodic chpple trussels remaking	1s.
July 7	Mrs Pearson John new Churn lid	3d.

He made waggons, carts, 'creadles', 'frail' handstaffs, turf spade hilts and handles, sledges, bedsteads, dining tables, quilting frames, a horse measure, cobbletrees, painted a new sign for the Cross Pipes Inn for 1s. and a refreshment board for

2*s*., supplied '12 stakes for dailliers 1*s*.' to the parson, and repaired an easel and made two new sketching boxes for John Talbot Esq.

The above joiners as well as others made waggons, carts and in some cases traps (*see plate* 242). There were purpose-built stone, wood, farm and carry waggons, and water, pig, bull, and ordinary block carts that tipped up. In the pastoral western dales of Yorkshire sledges and carts provided the means of transport, but because corn is grown, the dales of the eastern moorlands were waggon country, in spite of steep hills, for over two and a half centuries until the Second World War.

Before the eighteenth century the wain was the form of transport, and a pair of 'waynt blades' was a part of the body. 'A hundred years ago, perhaps,' wrote Marshall, 'there was not a farmer's waggon in the country.' Instead a wain, 'a large ox-cart with an *open* body, and furnished with "shelvings"', was used. 'Fifty years ago', he continues, 'wains were pretty common: now, there is not, perhaps, one left.'[1]

They did however survive a little longer in Eskdale and apparently resembled the Welsh wheelcar,[2] for although not to be seen at the end of the century (and none has survived into this), Canon Atkinson was able to describe them as two-wheeled carriages with long narrow bodies, the forward parts of which were shod with *clouts* (iron shoes) which when going downhill trailed along the ground;[3] and Mr F. Macdonald told us in his lifetime that he once saw in Farndale a waggon with wheels on the back and sleds on the front for leading bracken from steep hillsides. When pulling uphill the weight was lifted and when coming down it acted as a brake.

The dales waggon differed from the better known Wold waggon in that it was smaller and lower and had shafts instead of a pole. The body measures about 8 feet in length by 3 feet 7 inches in width, the hind wheels, with mostly twelve spokes, sometimes fourteen, are 4 feet to 4 feet 6 inches in diameter, and the fore wheels with ten or twelve, mainly twelve, spokes, 3 feet 2 inches to 3 feet 6 inches in diameter. Whereas the body of the Wold waggon used on flat ground is fixed to the undercarriage, that of the dales waggon is loosely attached to allow for play on rough roads. It was fixed to the wheels at the front only by a main bolt passing through the blocks (the top block being bolted to the soles of the body), spring pole and axle. At the back it was held by two hanging bolts (*see drawing on page*

[1] *Rural Economy of Yorkshire*, 1788, vol. II, p. 362.
[2] See J. G. Jenkins, *Agricultural Transport in Wales*, 1962.
[3] Sir Alfred Pease, *Glossary of Cleveland Dialect*, 1928; and *Quarter Sessions Records*, vol. v, p. 38, ftn. NRRS.

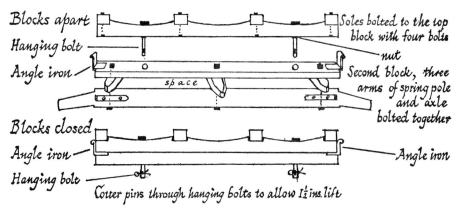

ATTACHMENT OF WAGGON BODY AT THE BACK. There were variations in the positioning of the angle iron.

107) and prevented from sliding by a heavy angle bracket bolted at either end of the blocks.

It may be inferred from an old photograph and an early child's waggon at the Ryedale Folk Museum that up to about the middle of the last century waggons had panelled sides, but the twelve which we have seen have plank sides (*see drawings on pages* 108–9). Although waggons were similar in general features, every joiner's work was recognizably his own—the front endboard and the number and design of the blocks lent themselves to variation—and each waggon was built individually to a customer's requirements, depending for instance on whether he had light or heavy horses. If work was slack in winter the building of a waggon or more usually a cart might be spread over a few months. A toy waggon was not uncommon (*see drawing on page* 108), and an entry in a Sleightholm ledger in 1887 reads: 'Thos Stanforth child's waggon repairing 10d.' By the 1890s 'patent armed' waggons, that is, waggons fitted with iron axles and brass hub caps (often supplied by the Kirkstall Forge near Leeds) were made. This improvement meant that wheels could be greased without being removed. Formerly the grease horn hung from the end of the spring pole at the back.

In 1844 a new Tomlinson waggon cost £25; in 1898, £32; in 1901, £33; and in the early twentieth century up to the 1930s the Harrisons charged £38 to £40. Mr W. Tinsley said that his father once made a waggon for a customer for £28, and that twenty-three years later when the man had a sale he made £1 a year profit on it.

The following entry in a Tomlinson ledger in 1898 describes the making of a

WAGGONS

1 Waggon from Fangdale Beck, Bilsdale, probably made by John Johnson (R.F.M.). 2 Child's waggon made by Daniel Speight, Church Houses, Farndale, dated 1836 (R.F.M.). 3 Brake shoe. 4 Naf (hub). 5 Jack, one of many varieties used for raising waggon wheels for greasing (R.F.M.). 6 Grease horn. 7 Part of shaft showing hooks for harness. 8 Waggon made by J. Harrison & Sons, Grosmont, 1918, owned by R. M. Pearson, Egton.

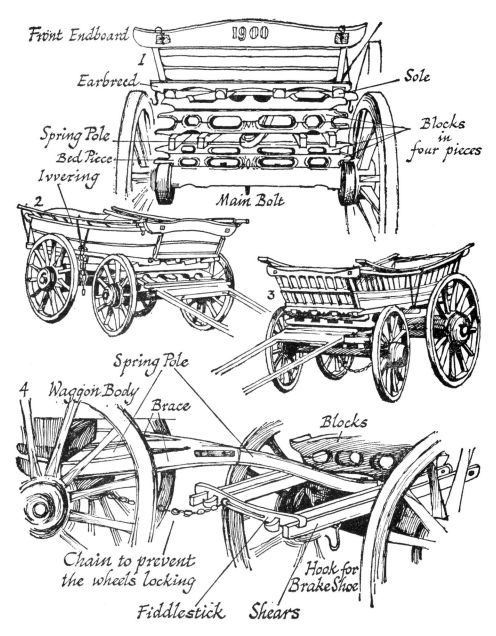

Front Endboard

1900

1

Earbreed

Sole

Spring Pole
Bed Piece
Ivvering

Blocks
in
four pieces

2

Main Bolt

3

Spring Pole

4   Waggon Body

Brace

Blocks

Chain to prevent
the wheels locking

Hook for
Brake Shoe

Fiddlestick   Shears

WAGGONS

1 Front, showing the blocks, of a now dilapidated waggon, made by Tinsley, Farndale (inscriptions on back axle) for Waind, Ankness, Bransdale. 2 Waggon made by Jackson, Duffinstone, Farndale, owned by Mr J. A. Aconley, Frost Hall, Farndale. The body is painted blue, the wheels and lining red. 3 Waggon with panelled sides, drawn from a photograph taken by W. Hayes at Hutton-le-Hole in 1913. The shafts are reconstructed. 4 Undercarriage showing the curved spring pole and shears.

new body evidently fitted to an old waggon, and the time required. This family kept patterns for all the ironwork required (*see plate* 204):

	£	s.	d.
4 oak soles	£1	0	0
2 Lockhole pieces 4ft. long		3	6
3 Oak hairbreads 3½ by 3 in.		5	6
2 pieces of oak for end doors 2 in. by 2½		2	6
2 Ash endoor quarts		2	6
4 Everings		10	0
42 Ft. 1½ in. by 11 in. Bd. for sides and ends		14	0
80 Ft. 1 in. by 5 in. groved Board for bottom		9	0
1 3″ by 6″ ash block		1	0
1 5″ by 6″ Do.		2	0
Carriage work & wheels 1 ct. paint		8	0
New boddy 3 coats of paint		12	0
Labour making same & laying on carriage wk. to same and painting up all work 2 weeks	£2	8	0
	£6	18	0

For making wheels before the bandsaw came in felloes were sawn out in the saw-pit with a narrow whip-saw, six inches wide, and then, laid in a *clove* stock (a small heavy framework put on the ground), they were dressed out with the adze. Before driving in the spokes with a 13- or 14-lb. hammer, the Dawsons used to heat them overnight beside the fire in the house, and every wheelwright fitted little hoops on the ends to prevent damage. When hammered in, the spokes had just to touch each other four inches down in the naf so that there was no pressure on it. The Watsons, after giving a priming coat, used to apply a thick layer of paint and dust sand from a large tin sifter on to the naf where the spokes entered.

Finally waggons were painted different colours: at Kirkbymoorside green picked out with red; elsewhere blue lined with red, and drab, spoken of as yellow. Wheels, painted different colours from the body, were often lined with white. The floor, made from green wood, was not painted. Waggon sheds usually had latted doors to allow the air to circulate.

JOINERS' AND WHEELWRIGHTS' WORK

1 Oxbow (Kirk Collection, Castle Museum, York). 2 Pig creel. 3 Two-man barrow (R.F.M.). 4 Pig tub for scalding. 5 Rulley (belonging to R. M. Pearson, Egton). 6 Block cart showing sword (R.F.M.). 7 Sledge (R. M. Pearson).

1

4' 10"

2

7' 2"

3

3' 10"

4

5' 8"

5

8' 7"

6

JOHN STANFORTH

7

4' 3"

6' 6"

Sledges used for leading peat and turf had either shafts for pulling with two horses or traces for a single horse. They measured 6 or 7 feet by 3 feet 6 inches, widened with rails, and with plank sides 7 to 8 inches deep and 3 inches thick with a shoe of holly, which wore shiny, pegged underneath the sides by three $3\frac{3}{4}$-inch oak pins. Sometimes they were further shod with iron, perhaps a cart hoop straightened and bolted on. Others of slightly different size and design but always with deep sides were used for transporting ploughs and harrows to the fields, for foddering with hay and leading bracken and turnips (*see drawing on page* 111). They are of interest on two counts—firstly, the great difference between them and the sledges of the western dales, and secondly because although they were once so generally used we have seen only two or three.

The Tomlinsons of Appleton-le-Moors, whose ledgers (with gaps) span the period between 1844 and 1924, at times went far afield, even to Malton and Gilling. The brothers Henry and George occasionally worked for Isaac Hartas at Wrelton and in 1849 made a new threshing machine for him for £4 10s. They benefited from the success of a local man, Joseph Shepherd, a shipowner in London. He built the hall at Appleton and his wife after his death erected the church, for which the Tomlinson family, including George's son John, undertook the woodwork, the wood for which was transported on the *cant* shown on plate 205.

Victorian life is reflected in the entries for repairing bells and Venetian blinds, for painting an 'Arabion room' at the hall and for '4 new turned Crokey balls and painting 4s.' In 1899 James Tomlinson, son of John, fitted up post offices at Appleton and Sinnington, the next village. The firm was often painting, lining, varnishing and providing new leather for traps. They evidently owned a seed drill and sometimes in the spring undertook drilling at 1s. an acre. Amongst a multitude of small items they made: boxes for girls and boxes for boys at 15s. 6d. each (for young people to take their clothes in after being hired), a 'New box to bake gingerbread 4s.', and a new signboard for the blacksmith at Appleton which with 'writing 22 letters and 2 Horse Shoes painting shading and varnishing' cost 7s. 6d.

BLACKSMITHS

'A good blacksmith could get a job anywhere.' Formerly an indispensable member of the community, the blacksmith working in most villages and most dales either large or small has gone within the lifetime of older people. Today there are less than a dozen in our area, some mostly engaged in shoeing ponies, hunters and Cleveland Bays, others in welding work for ships and modern farm implements, and a few specializing in wrought ironwork.

In the old days in summer they were kept busy shoeing horses and hooping wheels of waggons and carts, and in winter they laid pieces on harrow teeth, coulters and socks of ploughs—all repair work that has gone. Tom Robinson of Egton is remembered as a first-rate shoeing smith; the Atkinsons at Sneaton made 4,000 horse-shoes a year, and Mr Agar Hart, aged eighty-six in 1971, former blacksmith at Ugthorpe, as were his father and grandfather before him, shod thousands of horses at 2s. a set of shoes. Others were adept at sharpening mill bills, or tempering picks, or making masons' tools, many of which had a V-shaped inset of special steel which could be renewed.

Some forges had been in the hands of the same family for years. For instance the Swales family were smiths at Goathland from the late eighteenth to the twentieth century. They travelled round to the blacksmiths' shops on farms as far afield as Ravenscar. Eight generations of Pages had worked at the forge at Rosedale Abbey until the 1930s, and at Sneaton Smithy there have only been four blacksmiths since 1826.

Boys were apprenticed to smiths in neighbouring villages. For instance Charles Dawson of Newholm was apprenticed to Matthew Baynes of Ainthorpe and every weekend walked home the fourteen miles, whilst in 1908 his brother Arthur was apprenticed to William Allan of Grosmont for £2 a year. Arthur then worked in Middlesbrough before opening a forge at Egton (*see plate* 214). He and his son made a fine pair of gates which may be seen at the entrance to Stakesby Manor, Whitby.

Two other blacksmiths are remembered in connection with the iron-works or ironstone mines. William Hoggarth, born in 1838 at Egton Bridge, lived to be

100, and after work in Middlesbrough and at the furnaces at Glaisdale finished his career as the local blacksmith at Glaisdale End. William Champion (1869–1966), born in Rosedale, one of twenty-two children, also lived to a great age. He started at Sheriff's Pit in that dale and showed such aptitude for the work that he became chief engineer and blacksmith at East Mines. His son, Mr A. W. Champion of Castleton, has a fine set of brightly polished steel shoeing tools with hickory handles made by his father.

Another old blacksmith remembered is Job Bonas who in 1888, apprenticed to William Readman of Lealholm Bridge, had £2 a year and a fortnight's holiday to help his father in harvest time. He became a farmer, horse breeder, and blacksmith at Fairy Cross Plain, Fryup, and used to drive by pony and trap from there to Helmsley to shoe the oxen on the Feversham estate.[1]

The entries in a ledger for the years 1833 to 1836 belonging to William Milner, blacksmith of Glaisdale, indicate past practices.[2] From time to time he shod two oxen for 2s. Ass shoes cost 2d. each, a new plough 13s., two sickles 2s. 3d., a new turf spade 4s., a 'yettling pan cover and bow' 2s. 6d. and '1 New Strake and plates' 2s.—a reference to a method of hooping wheels with separate lengths of iron.

As well as work on farm implements he repaired the carriage of the parson and hooped a cask for the publican. He supplied wool cards, knitting pins, a 'Nife blade for a servant man' 5d., fitted a new complete range for £4 5s. 4d. and made *skellets* (small pans), *swittles* (gimlets), *hotters* (a plate on the axle of a cart), *tirrets* (the swivelling link of a chain), *cutwiddies* (the iron loop at the end of a swingle-tree), and was frequently *graithing* a tool, that is putting it together to complete it. An entry for '2 New Steeld cloutes and cloutes repair and mend 1s. 4d.' may refer to work on a wain, the front end of which as we have seen was shod with clouts. At the same time a clout could be an iron plate half way round an axletree. On another occasion he mended 'Waggon shoe luggs' (ears) for 1s. (*see drawing of a shoe on page* 108).

Especially when making waggons or carts, the joiner depended for his efficiency on a good blacksmith being at hand. Out of the £33 charged for a waggon by James Tomlinson in 1901 £8 7s. 6d. was for ironwork provided by Henry Harding, smith of Appleton-le-Moors (who also lived to a great age—ninety-four). This not only included the many iron plates between the wooden parts but hooping the nafs and the wheels.

The Allans of Grosmont, noted for 'their fine touch', worked across the road

[1] *Whitby Gazette*, newspaper cutting *c.* 1948.
[2] Lent by Mr G. Lyth, Lealholm.

WROUGHT
IRONWORK

220. *Mr Mike Hammond, Mr Wilfred Dowson and Mr Robin Butler repairing gates from Castle Howard at Kirk Forge, Kirkbymoorside.*

221. *Mr G. Hill making a gate at the smithy at Rosedale Abbey. He was apprenticed to Arthur Dawson of Egton.*

222. *Mr W. Atkinson, who makes and repairs ironwork for ships, drilling plant and agricultural implements, makes a wrought-iron stand at Sneaton smithy.*

223. *Mr John Rogers, Ingleneuk, Lealholmside, shoeing Old Nance, a Cleveland Bay. She used to take her master to the station and return home on her own. Rogers had blacksmith's shops at Lealholmside, Head House, and Fryup Plain* (c. *1900*).

FARRIERS

224. *Mr A. Dawson and his son, Arthur Dawson, shoeing at Egton Smithy (1959).*

225. *Mr W. S. McNeil, Pickering, rims a wheel.*

226. *He makes clout nails with which to nail the rim to the wheel.*

BLACKSMITHS

227. *Mr W. W. Featherstone, Lastingham, combines joinery with blacksmith work, thus illustrating the versatility of the craftsmen.*

228. *Mr J. T. Collis, Whitby, making a milk can. He rolls the tinned steel in the bending rollers to turn it into shape.*

229. *Joining the seams together by grooving a side seam with the hand groover on the side stake.*

TINSMITH: MAKING A MILK CAN

230. *Edging for the bottom in the jenny.*

231. *Polishing the finished can with Paris white. This shape of can with a hollow base is characteristic of Eskdale.*

from the Harrisons who were equally noted for their waggons. At Newholm one of the Dawsons was the joiner and his brother the blacksmith, and the former remembers helping to hoop up to twenty wheels in a day working until 2 a.m., whilst the Knaggs at Hawsker used to save up into teens of wheels then *booled* them a few at a time there and back to the smithy in the other part of the village.

Hooping five or six at once, blacksmiths employed a series of grates which they arranged in a circle with a turf fire burning underneath. It was not worth starting with fewer than about eighteen wheels; and Mr W. S. McNeil, whom we found hooping the wheel of a rulley (*see plates* 225–6) has done forty in a day. The heavy wheels of stone waggons and threshing machines were hard to manage, and the bevelled hoops of waggon wheels had to be placed first on the wheel plate.

A trailer or sledge stick, used as a brake on a cart when going downhill, was a simple example of the work of joiner and blacksmith. A shaft of wood 5 to 6 inches square and 8 to 10 or even 12 feet long was at one end shod with an iron shoe about a foot long curved on one side, and at the other end fixed to the back of the axletree by two loops on the axle and one on the stick, with a bolt put through them.[1] In another way a large wrought iron hook was bolted to the end of the stick and simply hung over the axle.[2] The cart was tipped back on to the stick, thus throwing the weight of the load on to it, and the iron-shod end trailed along the ground. Waggons were stopped when going uphill by means of a trail prod, a similar but shorter stick also fixed to the back axle, with a pin in the end to dig in the ground.

At Kirkbymoorside two forges founded by different members of the Dowson family flourish side by side. At the Ryedale Forge they were formerly largely engaged as farriers shoeing the horses of members of local hunts, and are now general agricultural smiths. At the Kirk Forge Mr Wilfred Dowson (1901–70) specialized in fine wrought ironwork. Following his father, who was a blacksmith, he reorganized the smithy after the Second World War, employing some twenty apprentices, and became nationally known.[3] Because of the many specimens of his work in London churches he was admitted to the livery of the Worshipful Company of Blacksmiths and made a Freeman of the City of London. His work is to be seen as far afield as America, Australia, India and Africa. Three members of his staff carry the forge on in the same tradition.

[1] Mr F. Dowson, Rosedale and Mr B. Wilson, Lockton.
[2] Mr F. H. Pearson, Sleights.
[3] See *The Dalesman*, vol. IX, p. 439.

BOOTMAKERS, SADDLERS
AND TAILORS

IN the sense of craftsmen starting with the raw materials of their trade and completing final products, almost, not quite all, of the bootmakers, tailors and saddlers have gone from our area. The first two groups have largely become retailers, and the saddlers, except at Helmsley and at Malton where racing stables and the hunting community are catered for, disappeared with the end of the use of horses on the farm and for transport.

In all these and other crafts lads served their apprenticeships. When about 1878 Mr F. Edmond went as an apprentice to a joiner in the village of Hawsker near Whitby, there were ten others; one apprenticed to a joiner, two to blacksmiths, three to cobblers and four to tailors. In 1845 Henry Swales was bound to Job Wilson of Helmsley, cordwainer (bootmaker), for six and a half years. His father paid £3 10s. in two instalments, the first after signing the indenture, and the second half way through the term. The boy was fed, lodged, and supplied with shoes and aprons, but he received no money except what he earned during a month when he was allowed to go harvesting.[1]

A scrutiny of early directories reveals that between 1820 and 1840 the number of bootmakers doubled. Although by the end of the century they were fewer, the many still working in the Goathland district, two at Goathland itself, one at Darnholm and one at Beckhole, illustrate the large number of these craftsmen.

Mr George Husband of Castleton recollects those days. Born at Rigg Farm between Sneatonthorpe and Hawsker, and one of a large family, he was apprenticed although never formally bound, to Tom Leng, son of Matthew Leng of Darnholm, for six and a half years. There were two Leng brothers and two apprentices working in the shop, 'a very little place with a cowhouse underneath'. At the same time William Stanforth, bootmaker and innkeeper at the Lord Nelson at Beckhole, also had three or four working for him, including apprentices. Paid 4d. a week for pocket money, George Husband used to walk the eight miles home every weekend. He eventually became a bootmaker at Lingdale near Guisborough where many of his customers were miners.

[1] Indenture lent by Mr W. H. Swales, Wombleton.

Adding to these, Mr Ernest Calvert tells us that he was born at Beckhole in 1885, but with his family soon moved to Greenend near by, and then to Grosmont where he followed all his life the family craft of bootmaking (*see plate* 234). Often working fourteen hours a day six days a week, he has 'sewn many a mile of strong boots for farmers'. The making of handsewn boots, then costing 14*s*. to 18*s*., ended about the time of the First World War. Ernest Calvert also made shoes, clogs, mended harness, and measured men's calves for leggings. These varied in length, and 'a little bow-legged fellow was bad to fit'.

The wearing of clogs also finished about the time of the First World War. There were Sunday and weekday clogs, and men on the farms sometimes stuffed them with straw to make them more comfortable. In the early part of the century Mr E. Moore and two or three of his sons were occupied for years making clog soles, and had encampments at Beckhole and in the woods of lower Eskdale (*see plate* 190). They felled young alders and sycamores and sawed them into lengths the right size for making two soles from a section. Split and shaped, these were stacked up, loaded into waggons and despatched by rail to various West Riding and Lancashire towns.[1]

Mr E. Ward, saddler of Helmsley, although past retirement age, keeps and uses the tools of his craft. His parents had a little cowkeeping place and he was apprenticed to his uncle in Helmsley. He learnt to make horse collars, the hardest work, using a collar-maker's palm, a kind of thimble held in the palm of the hand, and came to prefer bridle work, for which the best butt leather was used and the finest stitching employed. As part of his trade he sold the brasses and bell terrets with red, white and blue plumes for decorating horses on parades, and says that sixty years ago a complete set of trap harness, mounted with either nickel or brass, sold for £5 to £6 10*s*.

All kinds of work came the way of the saddler, from mending a fiddle drill to making dealers' purses to hold 100 sovereigns. These, with a flap, measured six inches across. Among the equipment in the workshop at Helmsley is a round stick, some seventy years old, and measuring 14 inches in length (*see plate* 235). One end was formerly used as a gauge for making the leather cap of a flail, whilst the other was employed when sewing the thumb of a hedging mitten.

Mittens were made from white leather, and the one for the left hand had to be strong to resist thorns whilst the other for the right had to be supple. Three thin metal patterns, kept in the workshop, for the back, palm and thumb, show the back considerably larger than the palm. When the mitten was being made, the

[1] Percy Burnett, 'Autumn in Arncliffe Woods', *Whitby Naturalists' Club Reports*, vol. IX, 22nd September 1945. Alice Hollings, *Goathland*, 1971, p. 60.

leather was wetted and the back bent over with pliers and puckered in at the top to sew to the palm, thus giving room for bent fingers. They were then sewn together with leather thongs in a running stitch. The left one also had a leather button incorporated, and the right a loop with which to attach them together for sale. The last pair, made about twenty years ago, sold at 5s. 6d. Edward Ward made us a flail cap which is seamed together with a leather thong, and a hedging mitten for the left hand—as nice and as functional an example of craftsmanship as we have seen.

Like their fellow craftsmen serving their apprenticeships, becoming 'improvers' and finally journeymen, working long hours, tailors fell into three categories. There were the 'whip-the-cat' men, small shopkeepers who combined tailoring often with that of a grocery business, and the better class establishments catering for the local gentry and the well-to-do farmers. The whip-the-cat man, carrying his goose (iron) and tools with him, including a damping rag—a square of white calico or linen or cotton pocketing—walked or drove round, and staying at farms, made or mended breeches, leggings, a suit or whatever was required.

Such a tailor was Pennock Newton who lived at Street, Great Fryup, and who in the 1890s kept a shop there. He rode round on a pony from farm to farm to undertake tailoring. Fryup is in fact remembered for its tailors. Others going out for orders and with several men working for them followed Pennock Newton. Travellers from Newcastle, from whom material was ordered, came by train to Lealholm and then went on to Fryup.

Sometimes hawkers selling suit lengths arrived. Mr R. M. Pearson of Egton remembers that when he was a lad his father bought three lengths, one for 5s., another for 7s. 6d. and a third for 10s. The 5s. length, allotted to him, was made up in Whitby for £1. At that time too the blue serge suits bought by hired men at Martinmas at £2 10s. were general wear. When in 1850 Viscount Downe had a gamekeeper, Robert Raw, fitted up by Thomas Horden, tailor, of Ainthorpe, he paid £7 16s. for a shooting coat, waistcoat, trousers, gaiters, a green livery coat, hat, girdle, buckle and binding. In the 1920s a suit of the best material cost £4.

Mr Fred Strickland, tailor in Rosedale for forty years and now retired, made suits for gamekeepers up to the last. He began his apprenticeship at Ness in Ryedale, where besides his employer there were a journeyman and three apprentices who sat cross-legged on the board one behind the other.

In those days lads wore fustian jackets and when he first went to Rosedale in 1926 he still made a few. Blacksmiths also liked fustian for trousers because it turned sparks. He made suits, ladies' costumes, breeches of riding tweed or cavalry twill for market wear, box cloth leggings and ones of corduroy lined with

232. *Mr William Swales, boot-maker, outside Rose Cottage, now known as Maryland, at Sleights. He won the men's race at the flower show when he was eighty-two. He was working in the 1890s.*

233. *Shoemaker at Helmsley or Harome before 1906.*

234. *Mr E. Calvert (b. 1885), bootmaker and shoemaker at Grosmont, also beekeeper, gardener and St John ambulance man.*

BOOTMAKERS

235. *Mr E. Ward, Helmsley, holds a stick formerly used as a gauge—one end for a flail cap and the other end for the thumb of a hedging mitten. He has made a flail cap which is on it.*

236. *Mr Ward finishes off a hedging mitten which, except for the side showing, is sewn with a leather thong in a running stitch including the thumb.*

237. *Saddlers at Malton making a full-size hunting bridle and adjusting a saddle. Chris McGrann, C. E. Barker and Dennis Newgent.*

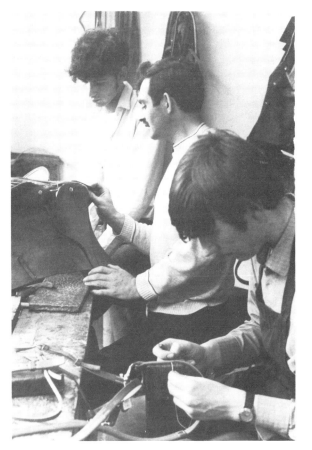

SADDLERS

cotton. Cloth, ordered from *swatches* (patterns) from a firm in Huddersfield, arrived by return of post. Besides local farmers, customers came from far afield. 'When I was sixty I could still sit cross-legged and bite my toe.'

Mr Arnold Leadley has described to us the tailoring business started at Kirkby-moorside by his father, Thomas Leadley, in 1886, and carried on in the same family until his son's retirement in 1967. Apprenticed to a tailor at Helmsley where seven or eight men were employed, Thomas Leadley remembered the first sewing machine arriving there and how they all walked round it marvelling, and that no one but the master was allowed to use it. As an apprentice he started by running errands, lighting the fire, learning to make button-holes and sewing on odd bits of material.

At Kirkbymoorside his father and later Arnold Leadley himself always measured and cut out. They employed a foreman, six or seven journeymen, that is men who had completed their apprenticeships and who earned £1 a week, and one or two apprentices. Three men or boys usually lived in. Sitting cross-legged and when necessary sewing by gaslight, they worked from 6 a.m. to 8 p.m. in summer, from 7 a.m. to 7 p.m. in winter, with breaks for breakfast, dinner and tea, and until 5 p.m. on Saturdays. There were jackets and breeches hands but after five years of apprenticeship a boy could make anything. The firm supplied all the tools except scissors, and seldom employed travelling tailors, who inclined to drink all Sunday and take off 'Tailors' Monday' as well.

Tailors always talked and gossiped, told and retold stories, and were given to bestowing nicknames on their companions. Breeze, Mitty, and Fred or Kiska King were some of them. Kiska King combined his job with that of postman, and having two or three hours to while away at the end of his round at Hutton-le-Hole he had a little hut up the moor road where he sat sewing waistcoats.

Thomas Leadley used to say: 'A man is very badly off if he doesn't get a new suit a year.' Customers, some for as long as half a century, returned year after year. Hunting clothes, coachmen's coats, knickerbockers, blue serge, clerical grey and grey 'pick and pick' worsted suits were made, and in later years ladies' costumes. One customer had three summer and three winter suits which he changed at set times, sending in the others to clean and mend.

Boxcloth for leggings, a material felted until an inch thick, was waterproof and as strong as leather. When the price of it rose to 36s. a yard Thomas Leadley, reckoning it as 1s. an inch, was disgusted. Calico had many uses, such as lining corduroy breeches and shirts across the shoulders—shirts in any case which came down to below the knees. The Leadleys sold shirting to make up, usually with an extra quarter of a yard for mending, which some old women added to the lap at the bottom. They also sold handkerchiefs for prizes for races, navy blue caps, and black caps for funerals, as well as hats. Once a traveller from Manchester proudly produced a bowler from one of his boxes. They showed him one exactly like it fetched from an attic. The fashion had come round again.

When Arnold Leadley was a boy he remembers that for the funeral of a large landowner fifteen black suits were ordered. It was impossible to complete them all in time, so the help of a friend with a large staff in Leeds was enlisted. Taking all the measurements with him, Thomas Leadley went to Leeds and stayed there until they were finished. Then the day before the funeral there was a railway strike. He managed to reach Malton, and there hired a pony and trap. His own, driven by an apprentice, started off from home hell for leather and meeting half way they arrived back in time.

238. *Mr John Redman of Benwell House, Lealholm, with a carry waggon, a waggon for rough use with open sides* (c. *1900*).

239. *Egton estate stone waggon, driver Joe Pearson, at the top of Egton Bank. The brakes on the back wheels were operated by screws.*

240. *Wood waggon crossing the ford near Beggar's Bridge, Eskdale, before the iron bridge was built.*

241. *Jim Todd (c. 1870–1930) carrier at Hutton-le-Hole, with his horse Pilgrim and dog Fury. Pilgrim ploughed with a bullock and was also ridden to hounds.*

242. *Mr and Mrs J. Tinsley and William, Low Farndale; wheel-wright and waggon builder (c. 1905).*

243. *The Helmsley fire engine on the occasion of Queen Victoria's Diamond Jubilee. F. Houlson is the driver with C. Allenby, F. and H. Atkinson, S. Barton, T. Dale, E. Baldwin, R. Magson and A. Ward.*

244. *At Ingleby Bank Top, journeying from Kirkbymoorside to a Sunday Camp meeting. Joseph Dowson is driving the first waggonette* (c. *1910*).

245. *Harome Sunday School Treat at Hutton-le-Hole* (*1919*).

246. *Small children on a decorated rulley at the coronation festivities at Pickering* (*22nd June 1911*).

OUTINGS

247. *Harry Grayson, huntsman of the Goathland hounds, calls them up (1911).*

HUNTING

248. *Tom Ventress (1821–1922) and Careless. He was whip for the Goathland Hunt and in all hunted for thirty-three years (1911).*

FOLKLORE AND CUSTOMS

THE north-east moorlands are places of ancient memories. Legendary tales, ancient practices, witch lore, and stories of hobs and fairies were formerly commonplace. It has already been suggested that many of these may be traced back to the early inhabitants, the Urn people of the Bronze Age, the proto-Celts whose settlements and burial mounds stud the moors, and as Celtic studies advance this becomes more evident.[1]

From these people folk memories were carried on into the Middle Ages, and survived as faint echoes into the eighteenth and even into the last century—longer than in many other districts. Fairies and hobs were implicitly believed in by the 'dwellers in those deeply retired and fifty years ago out-of-the-world dales', wrote Canon Atkinson.

Up to the early years of the last century the main amusement of people sitting round the fireside on an evening, or at wakes held for the dead, or at gatherings at wells on Trinity Sunday had been the telling of stories, and when this finished and people lost interest in listening, ancient lore ceased to be perpetuated. This significant change in habit, marking the end of an oral tradition, was recorded by Richard Blakeborough, author of *Wit, Character, Folklore and Customs of the North Riding* published in 1898.

We have been lent by his son, Major J. Fairfax-Blakeborough, some of his notebooks and two manuscript books, one compiled by Thomas Rogers of Castleton in the seventeenth century and the other by George Calvert of Kirkbymoorside in the second decade of the nineteenth. Calvert wrote, 'It therefore be a lasting and great pity that someone did not list to these old folk but regrets now be no better than a spent breeze.'

Rogers's book contains a record of fairies seen at first hand. On 7th May 1650 four people starting out from Castleton to Whitby saw many fairies at their midnight revels and when they heard of it 'This pleased ye townsfolk mightilie none been seen hereabout syn Dan Outhwayte was murdered eight year come

---

[1] F. and H. W. Elgee, *The Archaeology of Yorkshire*, 1933; see also Anne Ross, *Pagan Celtic Britain*, 1967.

Candlemas. Ye fairies were oft seen after thys by mysen as late as a week syn.' In Canon Atkinson's day they were believed in, especially as having been seen round the fairy rings near Fairy Cross Plain, Fryup. It has been suggested that fairies, not necessarily small people, are the ever-present spirits of the dead, originating in the fusion of the natural with the supernatural which was so complete in the Celtic world.

Hobs, too, mostly genial and helpful, sometimes malicious, had their own territories and names such as Hodge Hob o' Bransdale or Hob o' Hasty Bank. Rogers recorded that on 13th May 1694 Nathan Warner of Castleton 'thys day had speech of the Hobman that hanteth ye Hobgarth'. The most famous, Elphi and his mother Siba of Lower Farndale, distinguished by having names and noted for their 'deeds of kindness', are mentioned more than once in Calvert's book. In one story Siba is rescued from being burnt at the stake by Golpha of Lastingham, by enlisting the aid of fairies who summoned 'a countless multitude of hornets, hagworms [adders], pissamires [ants] which were thither gotten on the backs of great bustards, herons, skrikes and the like' so that Golpha was stung to death. Sibbe, but with a son called Hugh, was a recorded woman's name in the thirteenth century.[1]

Many of the legendary tales concerned maidens rescued from villains both young and old. One tells of a 'worm' being slain after hours of combat at Beckhole. 'Methinks few tales ever told', wrote Calvert, 'will ever beat' such stories as 'The Black Badger of Farndale', 'The Giant's Lapstone', 'The Fairy Cow of Wardle Rigg', 'The Hagmare of Orrer' and many others.[2]

Charms were prized as they were in Celtic times and in the Middle Ages. Made from skin, they are pictured in Rogers's book as having symbols of the sun, the planets and signs of the Zodiac, and to add to their effect incantations at the time of the full moon were recited over them. Rogers's grandfather, who had paid a crown piece and one of the best hoggs from his flock for one, wore it on his chest (and lived to be eighty-two). Another, a love charm, was worked on skin with silk thread by a witch Molly Milburn of Danby, who was whipped for afflicting a herd of cattle with the scab but who was also noted for her 'wonderful cures . . . never heard on afore her daye'; and another, a charm against witches that Rogers had from a wiseman, was hung round the neck of a sheep to protect the flock.

Witches are named and described at length in Calvert's book. Listing twenty-one in different villages, he says 'all these were at one time of great note', just

[1] *The Honor and Forest of Pickering*, vol. II, p. 153.
[2] See J. Fairfax-Blakeborough, *The Hand of Glory*, 1924.

as Canon Atkinson had pointed out to him houses notorious for having been the homes of well-known witches. There is little evidence of their engaging in pagan religious cults, rather they carried forward superstitious practices tolerated by the Church in the Middle Ages, such as signs and portents based on astrology. That some were women of strong *persona* feared for their magical powers is without doubt; many were unjustly apportioned blame for illness, disfigurement at birth, and misfortune, but it seems that regarded as part of the old traditional life they were not subjects for persecution.[1]

Both the gruesome ingredients of witches' cures and the gathering of witch-wood (rowantree) for protection against them had to be obtained under difficult circumstances. Amongst other conditions witchwood had to be taken from a tree never seen before. *Gads* (goads) were made of it, for one of the powers of witches was to stop horses in their tracks. People kept a piece in their pockets, and as already stated placed crossed twigs over house and byre doors.

Betty Strother, who lived 'ower by Castleton' and who died well stricken in years in 1775 may be studied as an outstanding sorceress in white magic whom men and women from far and wide visited for charms, love drinks, and cures for man and beast. From her mother, who had known Mother Migg of Lasting-ham, another noted witch, she had inherited a fund of knowledge, and she used amongst other properties a magic looking glass, a crystal ball, magic cubes, and a witch's garter. She was well versed in astrological signs and the complicated tables that accompanied them for casting horoscopes. She sold sigills (talismans),[2] small round lead discs, on which were cast the shapes of hearts, a skull, a ship (perhaps for a sailor), eyes, initials and dates, and which brought luck to the owner when travelling and for trade, marriage, births and deaths. Sigills may be seen at the Ryedale Folk Museum.

Amongst the stories told of her powers one describes how she could disfigure people who disobeyed her commands. In another she was asked to purify a butter churn supposedly cursed by the devil. When the powder she gave was thrown into it, a serpent which turned into the devil himself came out and made off. Serpents figure in Celtic mythology.

Wisemen at Byland, Kilburn, Nunnington, Helmsley, Kirkbymoorside, Lastingham, Cropton and Scarborough appear far less frequently. But this is

---

[1] P. Tyler, 'The Church Courts at York and Witchcraft Prosecutions 1567–1640', *Northern History*, vol. IV, 1969, shows that between these dates there were only three cases in the deaneries of Cleveland and Ryedale. See also Rev. J. C. Atkinson in *Quarter Sessions Records*, vol. VI, p. xvi (1888), who thought that fear explained the few cases coming before Quarter Sessions.
[2] See John Webster, *The Displaying of Supposed Witchcraft*, 1677, p. 156.

made up for by the wealth of episodes collected by Canon Atkinson and Richard Blakeborough about the wiseman of Stokesley, John Wrightson, whom the people from the dales sought out for cures for the illnesses of humans and animals and to learn of the whereabouts of stolen goods. His powers of clairvoyance startled many of his clients, who were told the details and circumstances of the reason for their visits before they had spoken.

During the last century tales of shape shifting, of witches turning themselves into toads and in particular into hares, prevailed. It was fully believed that many, such as Peg Humphries who lived at Piethorn on East Moors, were hunted in the form of a hare, and in this and other cases corroborative evidence in the shape of an exhausted old woman often lamed in some way found in her home was provided. Here if persecution was not in evidence, callous indifference was.

At Goathland there were three Nanny Peirsons, one following another and the last living into this century. A story told to us by the grandson, aged ninety, of the man involved goes that his grandfather once came across Nanny in the form of a hare and after hitting her with his stick he felt a sudden pain in his chest. When he bared it he found the imprint of a hare's foot on it, and in order to remove the mark and get rid of the pain he had to pay old Nanny heavily.

Another account relates how in the days of the second Nanny about the 1860s they used to play whist night after night at Goathland, and on one of these occasions a little girl who later became Mrs Richardson (1857–1940) and told the story, accompanied her father to a house. Nanny was sitting in a corner clad in a dress of blue and white check material that fell in folds all round her and with a huge flap bonnet on her head so that only her nose and a clay pipe as long as a poker protruded. Nanny asked the child if she would like to see her 'gan intiv yon cupboard' which was full of china, and soon Nanny became smaller and smaller until she was no bigger than a tiny doll. Then jumping into the cupboard she walked round and came out without breaking a piece. 'I saw this with my own eyes.'[1]

A recently used magic charm is an Irish Stick, of which we have heard of three —one again in Whitby Museum last used in Danbydale and another in Farndale last used in 1934. The latter is a stubby piece of hazel about 2 inches long with which a circle was drawn round the wound caused by the bite of a hagworm to effect a cure. It had never to touch the ground and was said to have come via Ireland supposedly from the Holy Land. In early Irish literary tradition a hazel tree was venerated, as for that matter a hare was of religious significance to the

[1] Mrs D. A. Sherratt, Goathland, and interview with Mrs Richardson, undated newscutting, *Yorkshire Evening Post*.

249. *Walk of the Ancient Shepherds Retreat Club, Rosedale* (c. *1890*).

250. *Rosedale 'Blue Ribbon' (Temperance) band conducted by Mr Mayman* (c. *1865*).

251. *One-man Band at Tate Hill at the foot of Church Stairs, Whitby. Several of the children are barefoot (date unknown).*

252. *Stape Silver Band, formed in 1885, at the Ryedale Show.*

253. *Kirkbymoorside Town Band, formed in 1859, at the May Day celebrations at Hutton-le-Hole.*

254. *Decorated horses at Burniston Show* (c. *1964*).

255. *Mr J. Welford, Miss Ruth Kitching, Mr E. Harker (blacksmith), Mrs E. A. Worthy (owner) and Mr E. Coning (judge) with Gillshaw Katrina, a Cleveland Bay winner of championships at Egton Show in 1971.*

256. *Mr T. W. Ventress at the Egton Bridge Old Gooseberry Show.*

257. *Mr J. E. Raw (1890–1970) of Grosmont, secretary of the Egton Bridge Old Gooseberry Show for forty-one years, weighing gooseberries at the show.*

258. *Judging geese at Farndale Show.*

259. *The Marquess of Normanby firing the stiddy (anvil) at Lythe smithy to celebrate the birth of his son (1954). A charge of gunpowder is placed in the hole at the bottom of the stiddy and is fired by the long rod heated red-hot at the tip.*

260. *Miss Dora Palmer of Whitby, one of the last of the vessel-cup singers. For thirty years she travelled from Skinningrove above Staithes to Robin Hood's Bay carrying a box containing a doll representing the Christ child, decorated with springs of box and sometimes fruit (1940).*

261. *The Goathland Plough Stots at the May Day celebrations at Hutton-le-Hole.*

Celts. The pig which, in the form of a boar, was their chief cult animal, appears in local ghost stories as a sow and her litter seen in Fryup Gill, piglets at Goathland and black pigs near Fadmoor.

About 1800, besides changes in customs such as the cessation of wakes for the dead, much was being condemned by country parsons, their wives and by the Methodists. Two games which easily turned rough, 'The Outlaws Bride' and 'Catch a Duck by the Leg', were forbidden, and a custom classed as unseemly was the race run after weddings for a garter worn by the bride.

Originally the race, competed for by the young unmarried men, was run from the churchyard gate to the new home immediately after the ceremony. The winner, kneeling before the bride who lifted her skirt, removed the garter, wearing it for the rest of the day in his hat, and then binding it round the leg of his 'own true love'. Often bridal garters were elaborate and finely stitched, sometimes on velvet. At night the competitors repaired to the inn, and drank in turn the bride's health with a garter borrowed for the occasion on the wrist, singing:

> The bride's good health we'll now begin
> In spite of the Turk or the Spanish king,
> The groom's good health we'll not let pass
> We'll have them both into one glass.

In the last century the bridal garter was supplanted by ribbons, silk handerchiefs, neck ties and money prizes run for in races, often organized events. The ribbons, 2 inches wide and a yard long, were worn as sashes; and we have seen a quilt, about ninety years old, made from twenty-nine coloured silk ribbons, which had all been won at weddings by Thomas Dale of Rosedale.

Old-fashioned funeral customs are remembered at Goathland. Up to about 1936 everyone was bidden, usually then by the family but formerly by the parish clerks, and up to 1934 the coffin was carried on two black crossed sticks by four or six bearers holding them in front of them and taking turns sometimes for as far as a mile and a half. Up to 1915 if the funeral was a woman's, women took over at the church gates, and carried the coffin by long narrow huckaback towels folded in three and passed underneath the coffin and through the handles.

F. K. Robinson in his glossary compiled at Whitby described the same procedures and adds that formerly children carried children and that for an unmarried woman the bearers, all unmarried, wore 'white with white straw bonnets trimmed to accord'. Where longer distances had to be traversed and often for estate owners, waggons were brought into use, sometimes in Victorian times painted black. In one funeral described to us as taking place in the snow the waggon was drawn by three black horses and the dray following with the wreaths by another, making an impressive spectacle.

Throughout the year everybody, guided by tradition, celebrated festivals, followed customs, carried out rituals, and ate special foods. In January on Plough Monday, the first Monday after Twelfth Day, old Christmas Day, processions of youths dragging ploughs went from village to village collecting gifts of money. The Plough Stots, as they were called, were accompanied by a party of sword dancers and Madgies or Madgy-Pegs, men with blackened faces and horns on their heads. Sometimes a guiser's play was performed. Young says that 'Egton Bridge had long been the chief rendezvous for sword dancers in this area'; but in this century groups have been revived and still flourish at Goathland.[1]

Amongst other celebrations, there were Collop Monday, the day before Lent began, when fresh meat was eaten, but remembered as the day when collops of bacon were cut and eaten, providing fat for cooking the pancakes on the next day. Shrove Tuesday. On Carling Sunday, the fourth in Lent, peas were the special fare. Nutty-crack night, nine nights before Martinmas Day, was a feast of apples and nuts.

At Christmas grocers sent gifts of two long candles, joiners gave logs of wood, and millers a pound of pearled wheat for making frumity to their customers. On Christmas Eve frumity, gingerbread, yule cake and cheese were provided. Yule cake was a plain plum cake resembling a teacake. At Kirkbymoorside a frumity bell was rung at six o'clock, and everywhere frumity, pearled wheat creed by soaking and simmering and flavoured with treacle and spice, had to be eaten in silence without leaving the table until it was finished.

Gingerbread, also called pepper cake or spice, a fine textured cake made of stiff dough on which a pattern was impressed, is well remembered and is still Christmas fare in some houses. The pungent flavour of coriander, one of the ingredients, may well have inspired the name pepper cake. Young said that the 'quantity of gingerbread sold in Whitby alone will amount to annually 12 tons', and Robinson described 'consignments formerly arriving periodically by shipping from London in numbers of tons. The manufacture of it is now extensively carried on in the town, and "Whitby gingerbread" has gained as great a reputation in the vicinity as "York muffins".'

From about 1868 to 1952 the Ditchburns made gingerbread at their shop in

---

[1] See Rev. G. Young, *A History of Whitby*, 1817, vol. II, pp. 880–1; F. K. Robinson's *Glossary of Yorkshire Words*, 1855; Sir Alfred Pease, *A Dictionary of North Riding Dialect*, 1928; F. W. Dowson, *Goathland in History and Folk-Lore*, 1947, pp. 95–100.

Church Street, Whitby. Nor were they the only makers. Mr T. B. Ditchburn has told us it was originally made with black treacle and latterly with Lyle's Golden Syrup and that there were plain and fruited with sultanas, currants and peel added. Some bakers added peel only. In the old days the dough was moulded by hand on a table, the treacle being gradually worked into a great well of flour. The plain, baked in hoops, had a pattern jiggered on them. For the fruited, cakes of dough were placed on wooden patterns carved by jet-workers with penknives and pressure applied. Between September and Christmas about five tons of gingerbread were made, all in different sizes ranging from 1 lb. to 8 lb., sold at 4*d.* a lb. for the fruited and 3*d.* for the plain up to the Second World War. Batches were sent away packed in tea chests, sometimes abroad to ships' captains.

At the Ryedale Folk Museum may be seen wooden gingerbread moulds used by the Sonleys, bakers of Kirkbymoorside (*see also Plate* 36), and the following is a recipe for gingerbread from the same town given to us by Mrs H. Coates, who calls her box a frame and has a mould carved in stone to press on the top. Her father, William Rickaby, a builder, probably carved the stone, and to obtain a good stamp he stood on it when it was placed over the dough in the frame on the floor.

6 lb. flour	1 oz. ground cinnamon seed
3 lb. treacle (melted)	1 oz. allspice
1 lb. lard or butter (melted)	1 oz. carbonate of soda
1 lb. brown sugar	1½ oz. ground ginger
1 oz. ground coriander seed	a pinch of salt
1 oz. ground caraway seed	

Kneaded by hand, all the ingredients had to be warm, and the dough was baked in a cool oven (250°F.) for three hours.

Lastly, keeping up an old practice far older than they themselves knew, the Smiths of Hartoft used to give the cattle a sheaf of unthreshed corn on Christmas Day; whilst the cat was offered gingerbread and cheese.

A seventeenth-century charm to avert witch evil and illness. From Thomas Rogers's manuscript.

SPORTS, GAMES AND PASTIMES

AS Marshall might have said, this is sporting country. Bells used to be rung at Malton for winners of the classic races, and game cocks, sometimes taken to London and winning at a royal main, were highly prized. At the beginning of the last century cock fighting, fox hunting, bull and badger baiting, rat killing and duck hunting with dogs were all pursued. At the present day fox hunting in the dales, grouse shooting on the moors and fishing in the rivers continue.

Hunting has a long history beginning with kings in the Middle Ages hunting stag in the Forest of Pickering, and the monks of Rievaulx hunting and hawking on their grange of Skiplam and in the grounds of Welburn. It has been claimed that the hounds of the Bilsdale Hunt were formerly descended from those kept by the Duke of Buckingham, who in 1686 spent the last year of his life hunting on his Helmsley estates,[1] and that the Sinnington was established about 1700 when the farmers of the neighbourhood formed a hunt club.

These, together with the Farndale, Goathland, Glaisdale, Staintondale and Saltersgate Farmers' Hunts, all continue. The last of these was started in 1939, whilst the Glaisdale began as a private pack of harriers in 1877. The many hunts have survived because hounds were trencher-fed, kept year by year by the farmers, and because the old-time huntsmen and whippers-in expected and received little monetary reward. The Farndale has never had a master. Huntsmen, such as Bobbie Dawson of Bilsdale, Jack Gowland and Jack Parker of the Sinnington Hunt, and Thomas Ventress, who lived to be 100, whip first for the Staintondale and then for the Goathland, are legendary names in the annals of hunting on the moorlands.

Trout and salmon fishing may also be traced back many years—trout in the Rye and its tributaries, and salmon, brown trout, sea trout, grayling and eels in the Esk. In the early seventeenth century men were brought before Quarter Sessions for setting salmon 'heckes' in the Esk at unseasonable times. Writing in 1846 Ord says that the river formerly abounded in salmon as far up as Castleton,

[1] Isaac Cooper, *Helmsley or Reminiscences of 100 Years Ago*, 1887; and J. Fairfax-Blakeborough, *England's Oldest Hunt*, 1907.

128

but that increased navigation at Whitby, the height of mill dams, and other impediments had exterminated them. Twenty years later when the Esk Fishery Board was formed, passes and ladders were made, hatcheries started and the river was restocked with fry. Sea trout and salmon now go up as far as Commondale. Similarly the Bilsdale Beck has recovered from the devastation wreaked on the trout from the refuse of jet mines.

Deep but not wide, the Esk is a difficult river for fly. One of its best known anglers, James Calvert, who lived at Lealholm Mill from the 1880s to 1916, once caught a trout weighing $3\frac{3}{4}$ lb. and a salmon weighing almost 23 lb. He made his own rods, tied flies and used the mill pool as a trout hatchery. About the end of the last century it was a favourite salmon pool, and crowds either fishing or watching used to congregate there in the evenings. Another well-known angler, Mr F. Edmond (born 1881), has fished the Rye and the Seph for twenty years and the Esk for forty. One very dry summer he fished in the Esk for eight weeks and landed nothing; on the other hand for several years thirty salmon was his yearly catch.

Up to about 1860, when they appear to have started to fade out, public challenges were a feature of local life. Men matched their prowess against other individuals at any kind of work or play that lent itself to competition; foot-races, singing, ploughing, mowing, thatching, stacking, carrying heavy sacks up granary steps. There were a Flying Clogger, a Flying Cobbler, a Flying Blacksmith, all prepared to pit themselves against others in races of 100 to 400 yards for from £5 to £10, races that attracted concourses of people.

Announcements in the *Malton Messenger* in September 1856 claimed that William Richardson could be matched to thatch and stack either against the Little Fryup 'Brag' or the Great Fryup 'Pet', and that the Glaisdale 'Swell' was willing to accept the challenge of the Castleton luminary 'Long Bob' and sing him or any member of the Castleton Brass Band at a contest to take place at Ralph Cross.

Competition of another sort was introduced in the 1840s with the formation of agricultural societies, which led to exhibitions of stock and of newly-invented machinery, which in turn developed into the present day show, of which there are a remarkable number in our area.[1]

Amongst them is the Egton Bridge Old Gooseberry Show, one of the last stands of formerly widespread contests for the heaviest gooseberries held all over the mid-northern counties, with a few in the south. Once so popular that a

---

[1] Besides flower and vegetable shows the following agricultural shows were held in 1971: Ryedale, Bilsdale, Farndale, Rosedale, Kildale, Danby, Egton, Whitby, Hinderwell, Sneaton, Burniston, and not far away the largest, Stokesley Show.

Gooseberry Growers' Register used to be published annually, they dwindled from 186 in 1861 to ten in 1914. The first recorded show in this neighbourhood took place at the Ship Inn, Egton, in 1843, and it was run as a club with rules, as it still is (*see plates* 256, 257).

In sheltered sunny corners of the gardens round Egton and Grosmont are nurseries and plots of young and more mature gooseberry bushes, hard pruned, well manured, and cosseted throughout the year until the great day of the show, the first Tuesday in August. Two varieties, London, a red, and Surprise, a green, amongst many others which have gone, have stayed the course for well over a hundred years. Mr T. W. Ventress of Egton, one of the old standards of the show, favours Woodpecker and Transparent, and with one of the latter holds the record for a berry of 30 drams 8 grains.

In the last century Egton Bridge used to be the scene of a long-famous tea party, followed at night by dancing held on St Thomas's Island.[1] In the 1850s the cushion dance (a round dance in which young people knelt on a cushion to kiss, popular in Elizabethan times) used to end festivities at Beckhole, Goathland, at Easter. It may be noted that some of the lines compare with those formerly sung in the same dance at Muker in Swaledale.[2] Even more ancient was the Kissing Ring, again a round dance in which young people chose partners to kiss. Two versions with words and tunes are 'The green leaves are falling' and the following:

> *King Henry was King James's son*
> *And all the royal races ran.*
> *Upon his heart he wears a star*
> *Right away to the ocean far*
> *So choose to the East*
> *And choose to the West*
> *And choose the one that you love the best*
> *If he's not there to take her part*
> *Choose another with all your heart.*

Probably the last time the Kissing Ring was performed in the Ryedale area was one moonlight night in 1930 after the Rudland Chapel Anniversary when some forty young people joined hands and circled round in a glade of trees. Flashes of sheet lightning accompanied the chant and some recalled the old belief that it

---

[1] *Whitby Gazette*, 11th July 1857.
[2] F. W. Dowson, *Goathland in History and Folk-Lore*, 1947; and Marie Hartley and Joan Ingilby, *Life and Tradition in the Yorkshire Dales*, 1968.

262. *Playing marbles at Rosedale Abbey (1908).*

GAMES AND SPORTS

263. *Sack race at Lealholm Sports, 5th September 1970.*

264. *Mr W. Leckenby and Mr F. W. Garbutt playing merrills on the corn bin lid at Sieve Green Farm, Bilsdale.*

265. *A league match, Beckhole versus Ugthorpe, in the Danby and District Quoit League.*

would ripen the corn. After a time the ring gradually diminished as couples broke away with the boys escorting the girls back to remote farmhouses.[1]

In Victorian times when they were formed, brass bands, of which only three of the many started up here remain, performed on every possible occasion. Isaac Hartas of Wrelton had a private band, perhaps a string band, which entertained the gatherings at his mell suppers, and William Garbutt, the conductor of the Bilsdale band, wrote a once popular hymn tune 'Ewecote'. Martin Sleightholm, the joiner of Goathland, owned a piano concertina and instructional and manuscript music books. Fiddlers, too, such as Ness Pennock, who played by ear, performed in more recent times at threepenny hops.

Although confined to an area centred on Eskdale, the game of quoits is still played. The Danby and District Quoit Club, apart from a gap during the last war, has been in existence for over fifty years, and in 1970 nine clubs competed in league matches throughout May and June and into July. Several individual matches also take place. Copper kettles once figured as prizes, as they did at the gooseberry show.

Quoits used to be played on the farms with two horseshoes *clagged* together by the blacksmith and with simple rules based on a series of circles drawn round the hob (iron pin); and there were pitches near village inns or blacksmiths' shops. At Egton smithy a set of quoits when not in use were put in the water of the slake trough to keep them bright. Quoits teams in the 1850s had twelve members, before the Second World War eleven, and nowadays nine; for 'There were monny mair young people about i' them days. Ah've seen twenty or thirty on 'em join up in a village on a neet ti play quoits, cricket, merrills or draughts.' (*See plate* 265.)

It requires a small manual to describe the many terms, the scoring, the throws and the possibilities of the game. A quoit weighs $5\frac{1}{4}$ lb. and the pitch is eleven yards from hob to hob. 'Hill' refers to the bevelled side and 'face' to the flat side of the quoit. A 'gater' is a quoit thrown so that it lands so propped up against the hob that it prevents a 'ringer'—a quoit dropped over the pin. A 'pot', 'quew' and 'Frenchman' are quoits that when thrown are reared up against the pin in different ways, and so on.[2]

Formerly blacksmiths made quoits for lads from horseshoes which were light so that they graduated from them on to proper quoits. Players carefully cleaned their quoits with sawdust after every throw; old men showed no mercy to beginners, and as a report of a match held in 1855 between a Malton and a Whitby

[1] Mr B. Frank, Hutton-le-Hole.
[2] Described to us by Mr G. Medd, Castleton.

club states 'the excitement was beyond description'. Although engaged in with concentration and skill, a game is now more of a social gathering looked forward to as a meeting of old and new friends.

Merrills, already remarked on more than once, was an Elizabethan board game, played generally in the region up to about the 1930s. It was either marked out on the lids of corn bins in farm buildings or took the form of a portable board with Merrills on one side and a similar kind of game, Fox and Geese, on the other (*see drawing below and plate* 264). Both are for two players: Merrills with nine plain and nine forked pegs, and Fox and Geese with one peg for the fox and thirteen for the geese.

Children's games and pastimes included all the usual ones and Coggs Off, Tip Cat, Atty (*booling* a ball into a row of caps), and Chequers, for which all had a mania 'kneeling down on our coats for hours and wearing down our fingernails'. Lastly a grown-up game was the Bull Ring, a ring tied to a long string and swung to hook on to a cow's horn fixed on to a wall or post. These might be found anywhere—in stables, even in tailors' shops—and the game may be tried out today at the Ryedale Folk Museum.

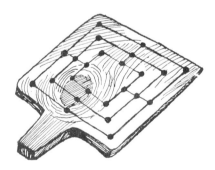

Merrill board.

INDEX

INDEX

Numerals in italics indicate page numbers of drawings. Photographs are indicated by plate numbers at the ends of entries.